A Travel Guide to Life

BOOKS BY ANTHONY DESTEFANO

ADULT NONFICTION BOOKS

A Travel Guide to Life
Angels All Around Us
Ten Prayers God Always Says Yes To
A Travel Guide to Heaven

CHILDREN'S BOOKS

This Little Prayer of Mine
Little Star
The Donkey that No One Could Ride
A Travel Guide to Heaven for Kids
The Sheep that No One Could Find

GIFT BOOKS

I Just Can't Take It Anymore!

A Travel Guide to Life

Transforming Yourself from Head to Soul

Anthony DeStefano

New York Boston Nashville

This book is dedicated to my friend and literary manager,
Peter Miller

FaithWords
Hachette Book Group
1290 Avenue of the Americas
New York, NY 10104

www.faithwords.com

Printed in the United States of America

RRD-C

Originally published in hardcover by Hachette Book Group.

First trade edition: April 2015

10 9 8 7 6 5 4 3 2 1

FaithWords is a division of Hachette Book Group, Inc.
The FaithWords name and logo are trademarks of Hachette Book Group, Inc.

The Hachette Speakers Bureau provides a wide range of authors for speaking events. To find out more, go to www.hachettespeakersbureau.com or call (866) 376-6591.

The publisher is not responsible for websites (or their content) that are not owned by the publisher.

The Library of Congress has catalogued the hardcover edition as follows:
DeStefano, Anthony.
  A travel guide to life : transforming yourself from head to soul / Anthony DeStefano.—
First Edition.
    pages cm
  ISBN 978-1-4555-2102-9 (hardcover)—ISBN 978-1-61969-659-4 (audiobook)—
ISBN 978-1-61969-660-0 (audio download)—ISBN 978-1-4555-2104-3 (ebook)
1. Christian life. I. Title.
  BV4501.3.D477 2014
  248.4—dc23
                                                                    2013043013

ISBN 978-1-4555-2103-6 (pbk.)

Contents

"In the middle of the journey of life I found myself in a forest so dark that I could not tell where the straight path lay."

—Dante Alighieri, *Inferno*

"I am the light of the world. Whoever follows me will never walk in darkness, but will have the light of life."

—John 8:12

A Tale of Two Worlds

Some books you plan for years. Some come to you like lightning bolts from heaven. This book is the second type.

One Saturday afternoon a couple of years ago I was at home doing some research on the Internet, and I accidentally came across an interview with a well-known Hollywood director, who was giving his opinion about religion. Predictably, he was an atheist, and his philosophy of life was one of the bleakest, most hopeless I had ever heard. He actually compared the world to a giant "toilet bowl" and said that every hundred years or so, someone comes along and flushes it (he conveniently neglected to mention who) and all the people living at the time are just washed down the drain into some mass sewer of nothingness.

This same "flushing" action takes place every generation, he said, and not only wipes everything out, but also renders all human activity and relationships meaningless. And, he added, since the universe itself is expanding and doomed to die at some point, nothing produced by humanity has any lasting value, either. The works of Shakespeare, Beethoven, Michelangelo, Einstein, etc., are all destined to be flushed down the same cosmic toilet—and therefore the highest achievements of civilization are really just as inconsequential and worthless as the human beings who create them.

The moviemaker concluded by saying that the only sensible way to live your life is to find ways to "distract" yourself from this terrible reality. Whether it's work, art, love, or sex really doesn't matter. The important thing is to keep yourself so busy that you never have time to think about the fact that "nothing means anything."

When the interviewer asked the director about the value of religion and spirituality, he just waved his hand away dismissively. Priests, pastors, and rabbis were all just "witch doctors," as far as he was concerned. Some of them might be well-meaning, but as a whole they were "dimwitted," "delusional," and "living in denial."

That's exactly what this famous director said. Interestingly, his comments didn't offend me at all. In fact, I thought he was at least trying to be honest and consistent. So many atheists today are inconsistent in their thinking. They deny the existence of God and objective truth and permanent reality, and then they pretend that certain things—

like "art" or "love" or "progress"—have some kind of value. But they can't have any value. Not if everything is destined to die and vanish into the black void of nothingness. The moviemaker was actually being very logical. If you accepted his premise—that there is no God—then the only way to live is in distraction. Everything else is just nonsense and self-delusion.

Anyway, the interview ended and left me feeling a bit depressed. I happened to like some of the movies made by this particular director, and I was sad to learn that he had such a dismal view of life. I felt sorry for him, and for all those like him who share the same black, hopeless outlook. But then something surprising happened. That evening there was some kind of Christian ecumenical conference going on in New York, and I had the opportunity to have dinner with two extremely brilliant clerics—one a Catholic priest and the other an Evangelical pastor—or, as the Hollywood director would have called them, two of the foremost "witch doctors" in the country.

We met at an Italian restaurant I like called Patsy's, on Fifty-Sixth Street in Manhattan, and sat down at my favorite corner table, where we proceeded to have a wonderful, warm Italian meal. The priest and the pastor were both in excellent spirits. It had been a busy day for them, filled with speeches and workshops and debates, and they were ready to just sit back and relax and enjoy some good fellowship. The restaurant, as always, was buzzing with happy people, excited to be done with their workweek, perhaps looking forward to a Broadway show or a jazz club later in the evening, and mostly just elated to be in such a cheerful place and to enjoy the delicious food and hospitality of the Scognamillo family, who have owned the restaurant for decades.

Amid all the laughter and gaiety, the waiter brought over some hot, crusty Italian bread and a carafe of good red wine and poured it for us. The priest immediately raised his glass to make a toast, smiled brightly, and said in his booming, jubilant voice: *"All this, and heaven, too!"* We clinked our glasses and began a marvelous night of good food and good conversation.

But as the Catholic priest and the Evangelical pastor were talking with each other, I started to think about the toast the priest had made. *All this, and heaven, too.* What a contrast, I thought, from the interview I had listened to a few hours earlier. What a difference in outlooks between the atheist moviemaker and these two Christian clergymen. What a complete reversal of worldviews. To the atheist, life was devoid of any meaning. At the end of it there was nothing, and in between there was just a random series of experiences—some good, some bad, some indifferent—all of them ultimately pointless. But to these two believers, life was full of joy—genuine joy, not mere distractions. It was full of joy despite all its pain and suffering. And at the end of it, there wasn't black nothingness, but rather, the brightest, most joyful thing of all: heaven.

Could there be a more stark contrast between philosophies? I asked myself. It wasn't simply that these clerics held a different worldview than the atheist—it was as if they actually inhabited a different world altogether. A better, happier world. But were they just "witch doctors," as the filmmaker had claimed? Were they just "dimwitted" and "delusional"? I looked closely at the two men sitting across the table from me and tried to be unbiased about them. The priest had written seventeen books. He had five or six advanced degrees—not just in theology, but in literature and philosophy and even civil law. He spoke eight different languages—fluently. He had been the publisher and editor of a number of well-known Catholic magazines. By any standard, he was a first-rate scholar. The Evangelical pastor was equally impressive. He, too, had written close to twenty books; he, too, knew many languages, including Chinese and Russian. He, too, had several advanced degrees. On top of that he had built one of the largest international Christian organizations in the world. Yet, despite all his accomplishments, he was a gentle, soft-spoken, and humble man.

I looked at these men and couldn't help but be impressed. Both had come from relative poverty. Both had experienced difficult family situations growing up. Both had known plenty of suffering in their lives. In other words, both had *lived*. They weren't naïve. They weren't "pie-in-the-sky" optimists. They weren't wishful thinkers. They weren't "living in denial." If anything, they were highly skeptical and analytical individuals. They were the furthest thing in the world from "witch doctors." And yet they both believed in God and in the possibility of true, lasting happiness.

I decided then and there I was going to write a book. In fact, before the waiter even brought the pasta appetizer to the table, I knew exactly what kind of book it would be and how I was going to write it. It would *not* be a book of Christian apologetics. There were too many of those already—in fact, I had written a few, myself. Nor would it be a "personal development" or "self-help" book about becoming successful. Those books could be valuable, but they could also be worthless. After all, the Hollywood director had fame, fortune, and a great deal of worldly success, but he was still morbidly unhappy. Why write a book on "success" if it was possible to achieve it and still be miserable? Nor would it be a book that pulled any punches. Life is much too short for that. Too many people feel desperately lost and alone. There's just no time to waste on euphemisms. Why write some long, professorial book that offends no one—but helps no one, either?

No, I would write a "how-to" book—but of a different kind. A book about how to embrace a joyful view of life without being self-delusional. A book about how to make it through this crazy world with all its ups and downs, and peaks and valleys, with your faith in God and humanity intact. A book about how to take practical actions and practical steps to transform your life from head to soul. A book about how to avoid hopeless despair and find true peace and happiness no matter the circumstances. In a word, it would be a book about how to really have "all this, and heaven, too."

That's the book I decided to write that night at Patsy's restaurant in New York City, as everyone around me was talking and laughing and eating and enjoying life. And that's the book you're holding in your hands right now.

PART I

Wake Up

"Some people dream of success, while others wake up and work hard at it."

—Winston Churchill

"You are all children of the light and children of the day. We do not belong to the night or to the darkness. So then, let us not be like others, who are asleep, but let us be awake and sober."

—Thessalonians 5:5–6

1.

Wake Up!

Most people are asleep. They're born asleep, they live asleep, they marry asleep, they have children asleep, they grow old asleep, and they die asleep. They're just asleep— all the time. And the worst part of it is that they don't even realize it; they're completely oblivious to the fact that they're asleep. Most people today are not real, living human beings—they're walking zombies.

Everyone says they want to be "happy." Everyone says they want to be "fulfilled." Aren't you tired of hearing that? There are thousands of books, magazine articles, and television shows on the subject, and the whole personal development industry is built on it. People today go around pursuing happiness as if it were something they could "obtain" or "possess" or "achieve." They treat happiness as if it were some kind of shiny, colorful toy that's in the corner of the room, and all they have to do is go over and get it.

But that's not the way it works. And that's why people are asleep. They spend hundreds of hours trying to look younger, or become healthier, or improve their relationships, or pay their bills, or achieve financial freedom, or buy that Mercedes or that beach house, and a million other things, and when they finally accomplish their goal—if they accomplish their goal—they're *still* not satisfied. And they wonder why.

They're not happy, because they're still asleep. They're still asleep and even worse, they're having the same nightmare!

Remember Pinocchio—the little puppet who wanted to become a real boy? That's actually a very profound story, because it has to do with the idea of free will and what it means to be an authentic human being. And it has deeply Christian undertones as well, because it's all about how we have the power to become children of God, and not just wooden, robotic marionettes. But do you know that today most of us are actually living the Pinocchio story *in reverse*? Instead of trying to become real, free, living human beings, we spend our lives trying to become puppets!

That's right, from the time we're born till the time we die, we continually attempt to attach "strings" to ourselves.

Some of these strings are material, like those we attach to possessions, and some are immaterial, like those we attach to places or activities or relationships. The point is, we're always tying ourselves to things, and the result is that we have less freedom and less autonomy—not more. We actually *want* to make ourselves into puppets.

How do we do that?

You've heard the expression: "Be careful about your possessions or your possessions may end up possessing *you*." Well, that's what happens to so many of us so much of the time. Whenever you buy something or use something or rely on something to achieve happiness, an invisible "string" shoots out from that "thing" and attaches itself to your soul. Whether it's a car or a house or a watch or a job or a person or a place or a relationship—it always does the same thing: it exerts a "claim" on you. Always!

By the time you're a teenager, you've got hundreds of these "strings" coming out of you, attaching you to hundreds of different objects—both animate and inanimate. And so you begin to live as a puppet. Your freedom to act in ways that are in accordance with your conscience or with the truth or with your deepest spiritual beliefs, are restricted to the point where you really have no freedom at all. And even worse—you're oblivious to it. You're a puppet who doesn't even know you're a puppet. You're a sleeping puppet!

Don't mistake what I'm saying. I'm not saying all strings are bad. Some strings are good. Some are even necessary. Nor am I saying that all acquisitions are bad. I'm not ranting against "materialism" here. I'm not proclaiming any kind of gospel of poverty or saying that it's wrong to be rich. Yes, it's true that people are too materialistic, but that's not the point I'm making. "Things" can be good. "Things" can be fun. There's a place for them in life. But it's our priorities that are all screwed up. Instead of spending ninety percent of our time focusing on what will really make us happy, and ten percent on the pursuit of "things," people do the exact opposite. Everything we do and think is centered on obtaining money, houses, cars, clothes, gadgets, wine, women, and song. I once saw a framed poster that said: "In the game of life, whoever gets the most toys wins!" That's the spirit of the society in which we're living.

Nor am I saying here that your career or your health or your relationships aren't important. Of course they are. Of course it's important that you care deeply about them. I'm not saying that marriage or anything that "ties you down to responsibility" is bad because it limits your freedom. That's a million miles away from what I mean. What I'm simply trying to get across is the fact that *none of these things is going to make you happy*. None of them is going to give you true fulfillment. None of them is going to give you lasting peace. It's all an illusion. It's all a big, fat lie.

They all work for a while and then they lose their power. The exhilaration you get from those trips to the gym, or from your lover, or from vacations, or from possessions, or from anything else that gives you pleasure or provides you with distractions, or makes you feel fulfilled, is just temporary. And eventually, when your health deteriorates, or you lose your job, or your kids grow up, or the person you're so in love with disappoints you, or leaves you, or dies, you're going to see clearly that it was all an illusion.

I'm telling you a simple fact. If you base your happiness on anything the world tells you is important—or on anything that may happen to feel good in the moment—you're going to end up being miserable. If you want to be happy, you have to completely forget about the world's standards of happiness. You're going to have to shoot for something higher. C. S. Lewis once said that if you aim for the earth, you will *not* get it; but if you aim for heaven, you'll get heaven and the earth thrown in, too.

For goodness' sake, look around you! Look at all those people jogging and dieting and juicing and eating vitamins and using twenty different kinds of skin creams. They're all trying to add a few years to their life. Wonderful! God bless them! But even if what they're doing is effective—and that's debatable—what are they really gaining? If they do manage to live ten years longer, does it matter if those ten years are spent living as a puppet? If those ten years are spent being fundamentally unhappy? If those ten years are spent being asleep? First wake up, and then worry about living longer!

The same goes for looking younger. The same goes for getting rich. The same goes for doing great at your job. The same goes for being a terrific parent. The same goes for "personal development" and "self-improvement." The same goes for finding the love of your life. You have to wake up first to really, truly, deeply, and *permanently* enjoy any of these things. You have to wake up and look at yourself and see all the thousands of strings you've got coming out of your soul, attaching you to a thousand different things—some of them necessary, some of them good, some of them worthless, many of them bad, and *all* of them temporary.

Do you hear me? You've got to wake up first. Life is short. Do you understand that you could be dead by tonight? I know that's harsh, but isn't it time we all faced facts? You could be hit by a car or shot in a robbery or have a stroke or a heart attack or a brain aneurysm within hours of closing this book. It's true. The same God that gave you the morning does not promise you the evening. Happiness is not about possessions. It's not about attachments. It's not about money. It's not about success. It's not about improvement. It's not even about human relationships. Those are all beautiful, but they're all secondary; they're all contingent; and the pleasure they bring is all dependent upon something else.

What is that something else?

That's the subject of this book.

2.

Get off Your Pity-Pot!

There's only one place to start a book like this. And that's to say, without mincing words, that what you need to do right now is stop complaining!

If you're anything like me, you probably get a lot of pleasure from whining and moaning and complaining. It just seems to be a common human trait. We don't have time now to do any amateur psychoanalyzing about why. It's just a fact of life. But it's time to stop. Right this very second!

If you're ever going to solve your problems—and I don't care what those problems happen to be—the first thing you have to do is get off your pity-pot.

Remember that scene from *The Godfather*—when the Hollywood singer, Johnny Fontane, goes to Don Corleone and starts crying to him about all the terrible things that are happening in his life? He has no money. His marriage is breaking up. Nobody is buying his records. He can't get a job in the movies. And all he can do is whimper and weep like a little girl and ask over and over, "What am I gonna do? What am I gonna do?"

And do you remember what the Godfather does? Instead of sympathizing with him or showing him any compassion (like many of today's psychotherapists might be inclined to do), he stands up suddenly, grabs him by his jacket, starts shaking him furiously, and yells at the top of his lungs: "You can stop crying and *act like a man!*"

Well, it's time for you and me to follow that advice.

And if you happen to be a woman and don't want to "act like a man," then you can "put on your big-girl panties" instead—or use whatever other expression you like—as long as it helps you to stop wallowing in self-pity.

Yes, I know that self-pity is sometimes okay and even necessary. All my life I've listened to people complain—and all my life I've heard myself complain, too. Sometimes we need to let it out. Sometimes we need to just wring our hands and bemoan our fate and cry out to heaven: Why me?

But not all the time. And not for long. And certainly not when we *really* want to change things. Because when we really want to take control of our life and turn things around, there is absolutely no place for self-pity or complaining. It's just useless. Life is too short. It goes by in a flash—for everyone. You just can't spend a lot of your time complaining. Believe me, you'll regret it. So enough already. It's time to *do* something.

Have you ever heard of the "if only" syndrome? It occurs whenever we experience problems. Instead of being honest, we say to ourselves, "If only such-and-such were the case, then everything would be fine—then I could be happy." If only I made more money. If only I had a better job. If only I could lose weight. If only my wife were more appreciative. If only my husband were more romantic. If only, if only, if only.

But you know what? It's all garbage. It's all nonsense. If you miraculously got a million dollars right now, I'm sure you'd be very excited and I'm sure you'd be able to pay off all your debt—for a while. But in about a year's time, I bet you'd have other money problems to deal with, or other family problems, or other emotional problems, or other health problems—and you still wouldn't be happy. You'd just be saying "if only" about something else.

The problem isn't with the specific challenge you're facing—whether it's finances or relationships or whatever. The problem is with you. *You!* Admit it already. Take ownership for once! Stop lying to yourself. Wake up!

I'm not trying to be cruel. My point here isn't to make you feel guilty. It's to make you get honest with yourself. Remember, it's not just you. It's me, too. It's everyone—

whether you're old or young, rich or poor, good or bad. We're all a bunch of crybabies. Some of the greatest saints in history have been guilty of this. In fact, sometimes the holiest people in the world have been the biggest, most annoying complainers.

Let's take just one example from the Bible—the great St. Paul himself. He was an extraordinarily holy man, everyone agrees. But do you know something? He could be pretty annoying, too. In fact, he was so annoying to the Romans that they eventually chopped his head off!

Well, just like you and me, St. Paul went through a version of the "if only" syndrome. In one of his famous letters he talks about how God has given him some kind of "thorn" in his flesh to "torment" him and keep him humble. He never says exactly what the affliction was—it could have been anything: a bad temper, a physical problem, a spiritual temptation, who knows?—but he does say that he begged God three times to take it away from him. He basically did what we were just describing a moment ago—he whined and complained to God.

But do you know what God did? He didn't console or sympathize with him in any way. Instead, he said: Enough! "My grace is sufficient for you—my power is made perfect in weakness." In other words, he told him to shut up! And after that stern rebuke, Paul didn't complain anymore. In fact, he actually began to take pleasure in the hardships and persecutions he had to endure, because he knew that somehow, some way, God was going to help him *more* when he was weak and suffering than when he was feeling strong.

And that's the same lesson that we have to learn.

You see, over and against the noisy cacophony of human moaning and whining and complaining that has polluted the earth's atmosphere since time immemorial, there stands alone the simple and quiet figure of Jesus Christ. And Christ has one message for humanity, one message of "tough love" for all of us. And that message is this: Enough! "My grace is sufficient!"

So you're down-and-out and can't take it anymore? You're tired of problems. You're tired of bills. You're tired of fighting with your spouse and with your kids. You're tired of being misunderstood. You feel that you're at the end of your rope. You just want to crawl into bed, pull the covers over your head, and sleep for a hundred years.

Okay, great, says God. Now we can start!

That's right. When you're weak and spent and feel you have nothing left—no energy, no resources, no pride, no nothing—then God can finally begin helping you in a *serious* way. As St. Augustine once said, when your hands are full—full of pride and strength and self-love—God can't really give you anything. But when your hands are empty and outstretched and utterly powerless—ah, then God can give you all the help you need. And your hands are free to accept it, too.

"But no!" you shout. "My family is falling apart. I just lost my job. I'm filing for bankruptcy. I've just been embroiled in a huge scandal and my reputation is ruined. I'm done with false hope."

"Enough!" God says. "My grace is sufficient!"

"But I'm grieving. I just lost someone I loved very much and I can't even get myself to breathe, much less function."

Okay, if someone close to you has died, you need to grieve. You need to grieve as long as it takes. You need to cry to the very end of your tears. And anyone who tells you differently should mind his or her own business. But eventually, when you're ready to pull down the covers and get out of bed again and venture back into the world, the same message still applies to you.

"My grace is sufficient." No more asking for signs. No more listening for special voices from heaven. No more looking for visions. Grieve as much and as long and as hard as you like. Grieve for years if you need to. But when you're finally ready to move forward, the first thing you have to do is stop complaining about your fate.

That's not being harsh. That's being *real*. Look, even if you're not religious—even if you don't believe in God—you still have to stop complaining and take ownership at some point. We've all read stories about people who have suffered greatly and yet have somehow managed to triumph over adversity. I don't have to remind you that there are lots of people out there who are in more pain than you—people whose problems are even worse than yours. We all know that there are children starving in third-world countries. There are people with terminal diseases who are worried that their kids are going to grow up without two loving parents. There are paraplegics and quadriplegics and others who have suffered terribly debilitating accidents. All you have to do is pick up a newspaper to read all the depressing stories about people who are suffering. And yet, many of the same folks experiencing these torments are able to remain optimistic and keep their hope and faith intact. Human beings have the power to "choose" to overcome almost any kind of challenge if they really want to. "It's not your conditions, but your *decisions* that determine your destiny." We've heard that line over and over from the gurus in the personal development industry, haven't we?

But just because we've heard it so many times doesn't mean it's not true. It happens to be a fact. Where there's life, there's hope. If you're breathing right now, then it's still possible for you to turn things around. If your heart is beating, there's still time left to change.

I'm going to try to help you to do that in the following pages. But for now, only one thing is necessary. But it's *so* necessary that if you don't do it you might as well just throw this book out. It's Step One on the road to transforming your life from head to soul. And in some ways it's the most important step because it makes all the other steps possible.

Whether you take the advice of God the Father, or *The Godfather*—please, for just a little while, take a vacation from complaining. For the next few days, even if you don't feel like it, even if every atom in your body cries out against it, get off your pity-pot, put on your big-girl panties, pull yourself up by the bootstraps, and *act like a man*!

Remember: "My grace is sufficient…"

3.

Be Honest About Yourself

So far I've told you to wake up and to stop complaining—and we've barely even started! Maybe you think I'm badgering you? I'm not.

What I'm doing is taking a chance. I'm taking a chance that you're really serious about life and happiness and the need to do things differently from now on. And because I'm taking that chance, I'm going to add another little "rant" to the list: after you stop whining, the next thing you have to do is be *honest* about yourself.

So many people today kid themselves about the way they really are. They think they're doing just fine, especially when it comes to their spirituality. They're not criminals, after all—they're "good people." In the words of C. S. Lewis, they believe they've built up a healthy "credit balance" with God and that, compared with all those other sinners out there who are so obviously bad, they're doing very well.

And comparatively speaking, they might be right.

But that's not what we're talking about here. Life isn't a game of comparisons. Yes, that's the way many people treat it. But that's also why so many people are unhappy. What we're trying to aim for now is honesty—radical honesty. If you want to be happy and fulfilled and at peace, you have to forget about comparisons with other people and focus on the truth about yourself.

And what is that truth?

The truth is that you love God, all right, until you stub your little toe! Then all the love goes right out the window!

We talked a few pages ago about how we're all complainers. The moment we're faced with a little trial—and I'm talking about a *little* trial—we start cursing and gritting our teeth and getting frustrated completely out of proportion to the pain we're in.

We're all so attached to our favorite little comforts. Forget about the big attachments—like status and possessions and sex. I'm talking about all the tiny things you hardly ever notice, like being attached to your email or your cell phone, or your Facebook or Twitter accounts, or your music or a certain TV show. What happens when you can't indulge in one of *those* things? How irritated and frustrated do you get?

I know some spiritual people who are always trying to give things up for God. Always trying to discern what they can "do" for God. Some of them have even left their jobs and their homes and their families and traveled halfway across the world because they felt God was calling them to be missionaries—to give up their lives and sacrifice "all" for him. And they were happy to do it.

But the truth is, one or two of these folks were happy to do it because they *wanted* to run away from life. They were tired of responsibilities. They were tired of obligations. What they really wanted was a huge change, a huge distraction. And so it was easy for them to "sacrifice" their present lives. Meanwhile, if these same people had to do something that was truly against their nature—like getting up early every day or cutting down on their morning coffee, or exercising patience when dealing with people who irritated them—they would get all bent out of shape and have a hard time maintaining their composure.

Maybe that sounds too harsh. I don't think so. Of course some people are called to do missionary work in foreign lands. Of course that's a high and heroic calling. But those people are a minority. And that kind of decision requires a lot of discernment. Before you go trekking across the globe to do God's will in Bangladesh, you had better first make sure that what you're not *really* trying to do is run away from doing God's will right here at home.

C. S. Lewis had another good quote about this. Remember, Lewis was one of the greatest Christian writers of the twentieth century. His books are famous for their clarity, their common sense, and their persuasiveness. And he lived what he wrote, too. He was a genuinely good man. Yet, in one of his personal letters, he admitted to a friend that when he really, truly examined his own thinking process, he discovered that "one out of every three thoughts was devoted to vanity and self-love." In other words, practically all he ever thought about was himself—how he looked, how he sounded, what impression he was making, how things were affecting him and his emotional state, etc.

After realizing how vain he really was, Lewis felt disgusted. But that isn't the point. The point is that at least he was being honest. At least he wasn't kidding himself. What about you and me? Can we do the same thing? If you analyzed all the thoughts that went through your mind during the course of an average hour, how many of them would be about you?

Not many, you say? I say, stop lying to yourself! If you want to put on a show for everyone else, that's one thing. But if you try to fool yourself, you're just a silly ass!

The late Stephen Covey talked about the three "selves" we all have. The first is our "public self." That's the person we show the world; the person we are at work, the one we display to strangers, acquaintances, and friends. That's the "self" that's always on its best behavior. Then there's our "private self." That's who we are at home: the person we show to our spouse and our children.

You don't have to be a psychologist to know there's often a huge difference between these two parts of our character. We all know people who are friendly and charming and funny to everyone they know, but the second they get home and let their hair down, they start yelling at the people they supposedly love the most. That's pretty common, wouldn't you say?

But there's another "self," too, a third part of our character that neither the world nor our families see. And that's our inner, "secret self."

The secret self is that part of our identity we keep most private. We don't show it to anyone. We don't even like to show it to ourselves. When C. S. Lewis admitted that a third of his thoughts focused on vanity, this is what he was exposing. It's what we're truly thinking and feeling in that inner stream of consciousness, from moment to moment. And the reason most of us would never reveal it—even to our closest friends—is that it's simply too embarrassing.

You know what I'm talking about. It's our secret self that feels all the pride and anger and jealousy and greed and resentment and laziness and envy and lust. It's our secret self that's constantly monitoring and calculating what other people think of us—i.e., how much they admire us—based on what we say and do. It's the part of us that's always looking for sex or power or status, no matter how much we may be smiling and what pleasant nonsense comes out of our mouths. And sometimes—hopefully not too often—these hidden desires of ours are so twisted and so devious and so perverted and so *wrong* that we can't even bring ourselves to admit that they're real, that they're actually part of our makeup.

And yet they are.

Now, the personal development people tell us that, to a large extent, our happiness as human beings depends on how *congruent* we are—how much *in sync* these three aspects of our character are with one another. If your public self is radically different from your private self, you're going to have problems. If your secret self is radically different from your private self, you're going to have problems.

And doesn't that make sense? If you live a life of hypocrisy, you're never going to be at peace. For centuries the greatest philosophers and theologians have taught that happiness is tied to the principles of harmony and balance. Well, how in the world can you lead a harmonious, balanced life if all three of your "selves" are so out of line, or—even worse—if they're warring with one another? We see this sometimes with political and religious leaders who are ruined by public scandals. When these figures fall from grace, isn't it always because they were leading double lives, lives that were radically opposed to each other?

Yes, it's possible through duplicity and lying to live in a kind of fractured state for a long time without getting caught. Some people are very skilled at it. But it's just plain impossible to be happy while doing it.

And to make matters even more complicated, there's an additional challenge—one that the personal development people don't usually tell you about. There are some people who can appear to have perfectly balanced and harmonious personalities and *still* be miserable. That's right. There doesn't have to be any conflict within them and they can still have wretched lives. The reason is that they can be mean—publicly, privately, *and* secretly. They can be nasty all the way through, and the result will still be that they're unhappy, frustrated human beings.

And there are people like that out there, aren't there? People like Dickens's famous character Ebenezer Scrooge. I'm sure you know some. The point is that harmony and balance and congruency aren't the only ingredients necessary for happiness. There's something else, too. And that something has to do with God and *his* vision for you, with the person that *he* created you to be; with the "self" that *he* sees: with your *divine* self.

We'll have a lot more to say about this later on, but for now the only thing that matters is that we're honest. The world is always saying that we're okay, that we're doing fine, that if only we loved ourselves "just the way we are," everything would be wonderful. The dirtiest word in the English language today is *guilt*. According to the world, all of us have way too much guilt—most of it caused by our backward Christian upbringing. Anytime we feel guilt of any kind, our society tells us that it's unhealthy and that we need to get rid of it as fast as we can. That's what all the talk shows advise, isn't it? They're always glossing over the fact that human beings really do act badly, that we really do think badly, and that there really are terrible things about us that need to change.

But we're not going to gloss over anything here. We're not going to pull punches or make any rationalizations. If you get one thing out of this book, let it be that you stop kidding yourself. You know what goes on in your brain. You know what you're thinking from moment to moment. And, my friend, you know that a lot of it is just garbage.

The same thing goes for me. The same thing goes for your parents. The same thing goes for your children. The same thing goes for the pastor at your church. The same thing goes for the president! We all know the truth about one another. We're *all* sinners. The good news is that once we recognize the ugliness and admit it to ourselves in complete, radical honesty, at least we can move forward.

And that's exactly what we're going to do...

PART II

Get Back to the Basics

"The way to get started is to quit talking and begin doing."

—Walt Disney

"Start by doing what's necessary. Then do what's possible. Suddenly you'll be doing the impossible."

—St. Francis of Assisi

4.

You Are One Person—Body, Mind, and Spirit

There are four basic, foundational principles that all of us have to get into our heads—not only now, but for the rest of our lives.

Long after you finish this book and forget most of what's in it, you're going to continue to experience all the joys and agonies that go along with living in this world. But there are four "starting points" you have to keep coming back to no matter what happens and no matter how bad or good things are; four pillars on which the foundation of a consistently happy life needs to be built.

The first of these pillars has to do with the "body-mind-spirit" connection, and it's what I'd like to concentrate on in this chapter.

When things are going wrong and you're not happy and not at peace, you can't just think that you're going to change

one thing and your whole life will be miraculously transformed. It won't, because "what's wrong" with your life is
almost never just one thing. It's everything. It's the whole
thing. It's all connected.

When you try to separate the body, mind, and spirit and
excel in one particular area, you might very well have some
degree of success, but your life, as a whole, is not going to
benefit—in fact, your life, as a whole, might even suffer.

Think of it this way: If you move your left leg in one
direction, and your right leg in the other, you're not going
to go anywhere, are you? You're going to be stuck in the
same position. Or if you're driving in your car and you try to
step on the gas with one foot and the brake with the other,
you're going to come to a screeching halt, right? And you'll
probably do some damage to your vehicle, too.

The same concept applies here.

You're a human being. That means you're a *combination*
of body, mind, and spirit. You're not just one entity. You're
not pure spirit or mind, like the angels, and you're not
pure matter, like the book you're holding in your hand.
You're all three, at the very same time. That's the thing that
separates you from the rest of creation. And all three—
body, mind, and spirit—are "wired" together, intricately
and seamlessly.

What's the practical result? Well, it means that if
you stuff yourself with food and continually overeat, you

might not just gain weight—you might also start feeling lazy, or spiritually dry, or sexually tempted, or you might find that it's easier for you to lie or cheat or lose your temper. The reason is that your body is wired to your spirit.

And if you read a thousand books in an effort to improve your mind, but fail to exercise spiritual charity and humility, you may end up knowing a lot of useless facts and acquire the reputation of a scholar, but underneath you might still be a hypocrite who's wrong on the most basic moral and ethical issues. Do you know any people like that? Any college professors, maybe? I do! The reason is that the mind and spirit are wired together, and can't be separated. If you do something bad to one, the other is going to be affected in some way.

Now, *how* everything is connected is a little difficult to understand—even for the greatest theologians—and could easily be the subject of a whole book. But the bottom line is that it has to do with your *will*. Remember, all the decisions you make in life are controlled by your God-given free will. Try to picture this diagram. On one side you have all your *desires*—the desires of your body, the desires of your mind, and the desires of your spirit. And on the other side you have your *conscience*—the knowledge of right and wrong, the knowledge of which desires you should say yes to and which you should say no to. Over and above both of these is your will, which acts as the arbiter and judge between the two.

Your will is constantly making decisions. Day in, day out, year in, year out, in thousands of different situations, your will is *choosing*. And the more you give in to desires that are not good for you—that is, the more you disobey your conscience—the more your will is weakened. The will is just like a muscle. It needs to be exercised in order to stay strong. When you don't exercise it, it shrivels up and loses all its strength. Then, when it's called upon to make tough decisions in other areas of your life, it's not able to.

That's why people are always complaining that they have no "willpower." They've lost it because they've made hundreds and hundreds of bad choices that have essentially caused their will to atrophy, thereby losing its ability to choose wisely or to stick to choices it knows are correct.

It's so important for you to get what I'm saying here. Everything is intertwined! It's all part of the same system. When you give in to one particular desire that's wrong— be it physical, intellectual, or spiritual—you weaken the whole system and make it easier to succumb to other desires that aren't good for you. And those other desires might be totally different than the ones you originally made bad choices about. When you weaken the will, you lose power everywhere in life. You darken the intellect so it can't see what's right. You disable the body so it can't fight temptation. You deaden the spirit so it can't resist sin. You de-energize everything.

You're really a very incredible creation—a well-balanced, harmonious, integrated machine—and if you screw around with one part of it, you're going to cause the whole thing to break down.

What this means, practically, is that you have no choice but to take a holistic, "total-person" approach to life, especially when it comes to seeking happiness. You can't simply lose weight and expect to be happy. You can't simply make more money and expect to be happy. You can't simply read a bunch of books—or write them, for that matter—and expect to be happy. You can't even just pray and expect to be happy. Even the holiest hermits have to get out into the open air and exercise once in a while in order to clear their heads. Otherwise their interior prayer life would dry up. It has to—it's a law of the universe, a law put there by God himself when he created us.

Look, you *know* this is true—especially in the area of morality. You know that you can't practice vice, virtuously. Let me repeat that: *You can't practice vice, virtuously.*

A person who embezzles from his job is going to be the same kind of person who cheats on his taxes, the same kind of person who is dishonest about money in general. A person who is slovenly and sloppy and disorganized in his professional life is also going to be slovenly, sloppy, and disorganized in the way he thinks—and probably in his relationships, as well. A person who is addicted to pornography is going to be the same kind of person who lies to his spouse and has affairs with other women. He's not going to be a loving, honest, adoring, faithful husband. And if you think so, you're living in a fantasy world.

Oh, sure, you may be able to get away with "compartmentalizing" your ethics for a while—cheating in one area and trying to be "pure" in another—but it won't work for long, and certainly not forever. The same goes for the other parts of your life that aren't directly connected to morality. Plenty of people have satisfactory work lives but miserable marriages. Or wonderfully fit bodies but emotional lives that are a wreck. Or stimulating intellectual lives, but terribly unhealthy eating habits. People function all the time in this fractured, compartmentalized way. But it can't work forever. Eventually your life is going to fall apart. It has to because the foundation of the entire structure—your will—is the thing that's been eroded.

And even if you could live that way, I'm not going to try to help you do it. This book is not about "functioning" or "coping." It's about happiness. And to be truly happy, truly fulfilled, and truly at peace, you have to be improving in every area of your life at the same time. You have to commit to working on the big picture—on the whole enchilada! So for the last time, you are ONE person—body, mind, and spirit. And that's exactly the way you need to view yourself for the rest of your life.

Make sense? Then let's move on to the second lifetime principle.

5.

About-Face!

How many times have you wanted to start fresh? How many times have you said to yourself, "If only I could begin from square one, everything would be different"?

But you can't ever seem to get back to square one, can you?

Well, guess what? You never will.

People complain all the time that they could solve their financial problems if only they had no preexisting debt. Or they could solve their relationship problems if only they didn't have so much pent-up animosity from past fights. Or they could solve their spiritual problems if only they could forget the guilt heaped on them by the church when they were younger.

Excuses, excuses! Nothing but excuses!

The point is not to try to erase your past and start at

square one. You left square one in the dust a long time ago. The point is not to begin at the beginning. That's gone. History. You're never going to see it again. The point is to turn around and *start over*.

What are the first commands they teach you in the military? In basic training, they show you a lot of things: how to keep physically fit; how to clean, assemble, and use your rifle; how to march; how to drill—and how to "about-face."

"About-face" simply means to turn around and go in the opposite direction. The sergeants yelling at you during boot camp don't tell you to go back to the starting point. They don't tell you to find the spot on the field where you were standing when the march began. They don't care where the heck you came from or where the heck you happen to be. All they care about is that you stop in your tracks and go the other way.

In war—and life can sometimes be like war—when you discover that you're marching into enemy territory, you have to be ready to reverse yourself. There's no time for soul-searching. No time for self-pity. No time for self-recrimination. No time for worrying about where you began or why you got there. There's no time for anything. You just have to turn your butt around and get going!

And that's lifetime principle number two. If you see that you're headed in the wrong direction, the first thing you have to do is stop everything—including your self-loathing and your self-analysis and whatever else you're brooding about—and make a decision to reverse the behavior that's causing you to go down that road.

Too simple, you say?

Baloney! It's not. It's the only thing you *can* do. It's the only choice you have. I'm not saying it's easy. Sometimes it's the most difficult thing in the world. I'm just saying it's simple. It's foundational. It's the only sensible course open to you.

You have to be really honest with yourself now. Is what you're doing today moving you closer to where you want to be tomorrow? If not, you have to stop and about-face. I'm sure you know this already. You might even know exactly what you have to do—or at least you have a general idea. It's not a case of knowing what to do. It's a case of *doing what you know.*

So many people don't believe they have the power to turn around. They've been through life's ups and downs so many times that they've lost all confidence in themselves. But that's nonsense. As all the personal development people will tell you, your past is not your future!

Do you hear? Your past is not your future!

Yes, that might be a cliché. So what? So your past is full of garbage. So you've screwed up a million times. So you're "damaged goods." We all are. It's impossible not to be damaged in this world. Practically everything the world tells us about values and happiness and pleasure is wrong, so of course we're going to be screwed up. And more significantly, the people around us are going to be screwed up, too, and they're going to hurt us as a result. It's a vicious circle. Get used to it.

Believe me, I'm not trying to give anyone a free pass. I'm only saying that if the morality of the world is going to pot, it's naïve to think that you and I aren't going to be affected in a very personal way. We're going to have lots of temptations and lots of wounds and scars. It's just a fact. As one Southern preacher put it, "If you soak in a tub of manure long enough, you just might end up smelling funny." And that's the state of society today. Some of us smell pretty funny.

So, what can you do about it? There's only one sane option—to move forward in the right direction. The problem is that you can't move forward if you keep fixating on what happened to you in the past. There's a great saying about this, too: "You'll never be able to drive anywhere if all you ever do is look in the rearview mirror." That's exactly how many of us live our lives. We spend all our time looking in the rearview mirror, instead of keeping our eyes on the road ahead of us.

Now, maybe you think *I'm* being the naïve one. Maybe you think I'm underestimating the weight of the emotional baggage everyone is carrying around. I'm not. Believe me,

I've got plenty of my own emotional baggage. I've messed up quite a bit in my life. I've done things I'm ashamed of, I've failed in relationships, I've failed in businesses, I've acted stupidly and selfishly, I've hurt people I loved, and I've had my own heart broken into a million little pieces on more than one occasion. As Frank Sinatra sings in the song "That's Life," I've been "up and down and over and out"—lots of times!

So trust me, I'm not claiming you can make the past magically disappear and reinvent yourself in the blink of an eye. It's going to take a lot of hard work and it's going to involve looking at the world in a whole different way. That's one of the purposes of this book—to help you do that. But the point is that you can't even start until you make a decision to turn around. And that's what we're talking about now. The *decision*.

My goodness, I know some people who have pasts that would make you want to cry. People whose children died in horrible fires; people who were physically abused by family members for years; people who were sexually molested in the most cruel and unspeakable ways; people who have lost everything because of their addiction to drugs and alcohol and pornography. I know one woman who had sixteen abortions! You heard me—*sixteen*!

Of course it's going to take time and serious counseling to heal these kinds of lacerating wounds. One of the reasons the personal development industry falls so short of the mark so often is that it's afraid to talk about the only kind of healing that really works over the long term, the only kind that really sticks—the healing that comes from God.

The Bible makes some pretty mind-blowing promises. It claims, for instance, that the kind of peace you can have if you follow God's will is so special and so complete and so unlike anything else you've ever experienced, it "transcends all understanding." The Bible also says, in one famous passage from the book of Revelation, that God will "make all things new." *New.*

This is deep stuff. It's not something you hear from armchair therapists or TV talk show hosts or self-help experts. God doesn't ever say he's going to take you back to "square one" or let you start "at the beginning." He doesn't even promise that he'll give you any big psychological "breakthroughs" in terms of understanding your past. In fact, you can search all of Scripture and you won't find a single verse that says, "Blessed are they who understand." Instead, what you'll find is "Take up your cross and follow me."

If you do *that*—take up your cross and follow God— then God pledges that he'll make everything in your life brand-new. He'll take all that's ever happened to you in the past—all the screw-ups and all the suffering and all the evil—and *transform* it into something else, something unexpected, something that actually gives you strength and peace and happiness. That's what authentic Christian spirituality has to offer.

But for those kinds of profound, transformative experiences to take place, certain other decisions have to be made first—decisions involving faith and repentance and forgiveness. We'll be talking about each of those in its proper place. But we're not quite ready for them yet. The only decision we're concerned with here is the one to turn around. And that decision can be made at any time, even if you don't yet believe in God or Christianity or the spiritual world. It's a decision that takes just a second to make. But oh, what an important second. It's a second that can literally mean the difference between life and death.

The best thing is there's time to do it right now. After all, you haven't fallen off any cliff yet, have you? Not if you're breathing. Not if you're reading these words. Where there's life, there's hope. Don't ever forget that! So even if you've turned around hundreds of times before, you still have to muster the courage to say: "Enough! I've had it! I'm going to do an about-face and I'm going to do things right for a change."

I promise that if you sincerely try to implement what you read in these pages, this time *will* be different for you.

6.

Momentum Is the Key

In order to properly understand the third lifetime principle, we're going to have to do some physics. Remember physics from school? Remember all the "laws" of the universe? The law of gravity? The law of conservation of matter and energy?

Well, there was another law they taught us that's absolutely essential if we want to understand why life can be so unhappy and why it can be so difficult to change. It's called the *law of inertia.*

Do you recall what this law states? "An object at rest tends to stay at rest."

If a car is parked on the street with the engine turned off, it's not going to move anywhere—at least not on its own. It's going to stay right there. If a chair is placed next to a desk and no one touches it, it's going to remain in that position gathering dust till kingdom come. Things don't just move by themselves unless something *makes* them move. That couldn't be more simple, right?

But guess what? The law of inertia isn't only true in physics. It's true in every area of life. It's true for human beings. It's true for businesses. It's true for governments. It's especially true for people who are experiencing different kinds of "funks." When you're overweight and out of shape, you're essentially "at rest," and tend to "stay at rest." You don't want to go to the gym and exercise, or lift weights, or run. When you're disorganized and sloppy and your life is a big mess, you're "at rest" and tend to "stay at rest." You don't want to straighten everything up or do a major house cleaning. When your finances are in shambles and you owe everybody money, you're "at rest" and tend to "stay at rest." You don't want to make the hard choices necessary to correct the situation. You don't want to cut your expenses drastically or stop using your credit cards. You don't want to even look at your bills. Instead you want to watch TV, or have a drink, or eat, or gamble, or play video games, or go on vacation, or have sex. Anything to distract you from your problems.

Why? Because nobody wants pain! Looking at a balance sheet when we know our finances are a wreck is painful. Looking in the mirror when we're disgusted with all our flab is painful. The only time we actually get off our butts and take action is when the pain of *not* doing something becomes so great that it exceeds the pain of doing it. In other words, we sometimes get *so* upset by the way things are that it's enough to actually push ourselves *through* the pain and *move*.

One of the personal development experts—I think it was Tony Robbins—called this phenomenon the "pressure cooker." We indulge in behavior that isn't good for us and as a result, bad things start to happen. This causes us to feel pain and we have the desire to change—but the effort required is too difficult, so we don't. Instead the pressure builds and builds until it gets so great that we *have to* do something—otherwise there would be an explosion. But then, once we finally take action and things start to improve, the pressure lets off for a while—and guess what happens? We start the same old bad behavior again. Almost immediately, the pressure begins to build. And so we go through the process over and over again.

Is that your life? A pressure cooker? Is that the way you want to spend the tiny amount of time you have on this planet?

Listen, there's a better way to get yourself to move, a better way to overcome the law of inertia—one that doesn't require explosive pressure. And it actually involves another principle from physics. It's called *momentum*.

Follow me here! This is one of the most important

things in life to learn. And it's so simple that people forget it all the time. When an object at rest starts to move, it moves slowly at first. It doesn't just go at full speed instantaneously. It accelerates. It *builds* momentum. I've done a lot of traveling on planes in my life. In fact, I happen to be a pilot. When you're on the runway and you begin your take-off roll, you don't just miraculously lift off the ground. You wait for the tower to say, "Clear for takeoff." Then you push the throttle forward and the plane begins to inch along. At first you're going very slowly—so slowly that a child could easily outrun you. Then, as the seconds tick by, your speed picks up, and before you know it, you're airborne.

This is true for everything in life.

The key to taking effective, long-lasting action is momentum. If you want to get out of a funk—any funk—the best thing to do is to start with small actions, even the tiniest ones, but to take them consistently over the period of a few days and weeks. Once you do that, things are bound to accelerate.

You *know* this works. You've been through it before. You know that first trip to the gym is the hardest. It's actually torture to force yourself to go. The second trip is a little easier. The third easier still. By the fourth time, you're raring to go. In fact, nothing can stop you from going. The same applies to getting yourself organized. Or straightening out your finances. Or even fixing your relationships. If you start small and force yourself through the initial period of pain, you *will* pick up speed. It's just a law of the universe.

And even if it took longer than you expected to build momentum, small steps would still be the key to success. I don't care how cliché this sounds, but slow and steady always wins the race. Always.

Ernest Hemingway was one of the greatest writers who ever lived. His novels and short stories changed literature forever. But do you know how much he wrote a day? A mere 250 words! Once in a while he got lucky and was able to write five hundred. But that was rare. In all his years of writing, he never cared about putting thousands of words down on paper, as so many other authors do. He just wanted to write "a good 250." But he wanted to do it consistently. He knew that if he did that every day, he would have a whole book by the end of the year.

Do you realize that? Do you realize that if you wrote a steady 250 words a day, you could have a novel done within twelve months?

We've all got to get off this roller coaster we're on. Up and down, up and down. It never stops. How many "phases" have you gone through in your life? We're always going through "phases." Isn't it pathetic? We're always getting excited about this thing or that. Always trying some fad diet or exercise plan or personal development program. They all work for a while but then lose their power once the emotional high is gone. We're like dumb mice that keep going for the same piece of cheese in the same mousetrap, no matter how many times we get caught. Aren't you tired of it?

But if you start small and build slowly—or even if you just keep up the same pace—your progress won't stop with such depressing regularity. Life won't be a roller coaster or a pressure cooker or a series of phases anymore. Wouldn't that be nice?

This isn't just some personal development principle. It's at the heart of true spirituality. The Bible says, "Do not despise small beginnings." And if you look through Scripture, you'll find dozens of examples of battles in which a small handful of warriors was able to miraculously defeat a huge army. God always seems to go out of his way to show that small numbers of people—or even people of small stature— have the power to overcome overwhelming odds, as long as he is on their side.

The best example of this, of course, is the story of how God saved humanity. Now, nothing is bigger or greater or more powerful than God, right? And yet, when this same Almighty God chose to enter human history and become a man, he did so by first becoming a little baby. We can't ever forget that Jesus Christ—who Christians believe *is* God— was born a child in a small manger. And before that he was an embryo in his mother's womb. And before that he was a zygote—just two cells, yet divine! Consider the implica-tions! If God himself thought it was best to start small, why wouldn't we use the same strategy?

Building momentum always works. It doesn't matter if you're eighteen or eighty, broke or a billionaire, the worst sinner in the world or the greatest saint. Sometimes the re-sults aren't always immediate, but that's to be expected. You don't plant seeds at night and expect flowers to be blooming the next morning, do you? It takes time before you can reap what you sow. But you've got to start sowing. You've got to get the seeds in the ground!

If you're in lousy physical shape and need to start an exercise routine, of course it would be great if you could start going to the gym regularly. But if you can't bring yourself to do that right now, fine. Just go take a walk around the block instead. Or drink a few extra glasses of water. Or buy an exercise book and read the first chapter. It's not really important what you do as long as you do *something*—and as long as you *keep* doing a little some-thing every day.

Or if your life is a chaotic mess, then go ahead and start organizing a tiny part of it. Go clean your closet! Who cares if some people think that's silly? Who cares if it's a cliché? Who cares if you've got much bigger concerns? The point is that it works. It gets the juices flowing. It gives you the feeling that you're in control of your life—and that's something that's absolutely necessary if you're ever going to solve all your other problems.

Remember, this is just a starting point. But it's a starting point we've got to keep coming back to. Gravity is always going to be pulling us down. Stumbling blocks are always going to be thrust in our way. And when we run across them and they halt our progress, we've got to be able to jump-start ourselves with a minimum amount of turmoil. No more pressure cooker! Whether it's our bodies, our minds, or our spirits we're working on, it's always best to take baby steps first.

Of course you have to get radical, too. It's impossible to be happy if you're not radical in your approach to life and in your approach to God. We said in the very first chapter that you can have great health, great relationships, and a billion dollars, and still be a slave to your attachments and a miserable wretch. We're going to address all that, don't worry. But at this stage it's better to just concentrate on *moving*.

So don't despise small beginnings! Pick a few random things right now—a few nagging tasks, a few irritating to-do items you haven't been able to get done in the last few months—and start working on them, slowly. Resist the urge to do it all at once. Consistency is what we're aiming for. Momentum is what we're aiming for.

Go do something small!

7.

Personal Development
Is Not Enough

The fourth basic lifetime principle we're going to discuss has to do with the G-word. *God.*

Now, I've mentioned God and Christianity and the Bible in this book, but not really that much. I certainly haven't beaten you over the head with religion, have I?

The reason is *not* that it's not important. It's that it's *so* important I didn't want you to just dismiss what I was saying because you happen to be an atheist or an agnostic, or because you're angry at God or the church or at "organized religion" in general.

Nowadays people hear you say the word *God* and they get so nervous. They automatically think you're going to start preaching to them. Well, I'm not a preacher. But I *am* going to give you a little sermon right now on the truth about life. In fact, it may be the most important sermon you'll ever hear. And I don't intend to dilute it or sugarcoat it in any way. I'm just going to give it to you straight.

If you think you're going to make it through this crazy, schizophrenic world of ours, with all its ups and downs and pains and pleasures, and somehow manage to experience peace and happiness without paying any attention to what God wants from you, you're really kidding yourself. I don't care how successful you are or how many personal development courses you've taken or how much you think you've got it all together; the moment life really slams you in the face with a two-by-four (and if it hasn't already, trust me, it will) your whole pretty, phony, fragile façade of "contentment" is going to come crumbling down.

And not only that, but even if nothing bad ever happens to you (and I hope it doesn't), you *still* wouldn't get anywhere near true peace and happiness. Notice I didn't say you couldn't make lots of money and have lots of pleasures and lots of sexy distractions. Nor did I say that you couldn't have lots of wonderful, loving experiences with your family and friends. I said you couldn't get to true peace and happiness. Unless you understand what those terms really mean, and unless you understand how following God's plan will get you there, you're never going to understand why so many people fail in their quest to attain them.

Think about a map for a minute. Stephen Covey, who wrote the bestselling book *The 7 Habits of Highly Effective*

People, made a great point about maps. He said that if you wanted to get to a certain place in New York City but had never been there before, you might go out and buy one of those cheap maps they sell on the street. But what if there had been an error in the printing of the map? What if the mapmaker had accidentally labeled the map "New York City," when it was really a map of Chicago?

If you tried to follow that map, it would be pretty confusing, wouldn't it? You'd try to go down the right streets and make the correct turns, but you'd keep ending up at the wrong place. You'd go in a bunch of different directions but you'd still be lost. And yet, if you looked down at the map it would say very clearly, "New York City."

That's exactly what our society has done to people today. It's given us a map that's labeled "Happiness" and urged us to follow it. Only it's not a map to Happiness at all. It's a map to "Success" or to "Self-Improvement" or to "Worldly Pleasures" or to "Sex Without Responsibility" or to "Style and Cool," or to God knows what. Most times, it just ends up being a map to "Misery." But the wrong label has been stuck on it, and it's been sold to us anyway. And like sheep, we blindly follow it, and then scratch our heads and wonder why we never arrive at our destination.

Well there *is* an accurate map that exists. And it's the map that's been provided to us by God himself in the form of his Ten Commandments, his Laws, his Word, and primarily the church he founded—Christianity. This map has one main destination—heaven. And surprisingly, God has made the gigantic claim that if you follow this map and attempt to reach that destination, you'll actually experience peace and happiness *along the way*. Therefore, it's a map that gives you two destinations for the price of one: heaven in the world to come, and peace and happiness right now.

Now, a lot of people don't like this map. Some don't believe it to begin with. Others just find it too difficult to follow. After all, it doesn't exactly provide us with the "easiest" route of passage. In fact, it takes us through some pretty rough terrain. Some of the roads are rocky and winding and pretty scary. And it often leads us through climates that are dark and stormy. The map promises peace and happiness, but paradoxically, it also promises that we have to suffer and in the process might even be persecuted. People don't want to hear that, do they?

But at least it's a map that claims to be true, and at least it's one that's accurately labeled. We may not always like what it says, but it's not false advertising. Not according to the mapmaker, anyway.

The same can't be said for all the empty promises the culture tries to ram down our throats about sex and money and power and status. Even the personal development industry—which I genuinely respect because it tries to help people—is guilty of the same defective labeling. It says it wants to assist us to make improvements in our lives, but then it leaves out the most important factor in determining what true "improvement" really depends on: following God's map.

Self-help experts claim that they can teach us to control the way we think and focus on the "positive," thereby making us more efficient, effective, and optimistic. They say that the way we think about things determines our emotional state, and that therefore even the worst experiences can yield the best results, if we view them as "opportunities for growth."

Wonderful! All of those famous personal development books—*As a Man Thinketh*, *How to Win Friends and Influence People*, *Think and Grow Rich*, *Awaken the Giant Within*, etc., are terrific. God bless them, every one.

But they all have the same weakness, the same Achilles' heel. They all fail to take into account the presence of God and *his* plan for us. Because of that, none of them has the slightest clue how to teach us to live truly good, holy lives— the kind God wants us to live.

Let's use a very extreme example. If Adolf Hitler had somehow been able to take a personal development course during World War II, he wouldn't have done one thing differently to change his own character or his own monstrous morality—he would just have become a happier, more efficient Adolf Hitler. Let me repeat that. If self-help books and audio programs and seminars were available back in the 1940s, and Adolf Hitler made full use of them, he would simply have become a better version of his evil self!

Now, please don't misunderstand me. I'm not comparing personal development experts to the Nazis. Nor am I saying that if you follow a self-improvement program it's going to make you evil. It's not. I've used self-help books and audios for years and benefited greatly from them. I love them. But what I'm saying now is that they're not enough. They're deficient. In the hands of someone who's selfish or cruel or evil, they can actually do more damage than good.

The biggest problem with much of the personal development industry is that it's *devoid* of any real moral compass. So many of today's self-help gurus are so worried that they're going to come off as too "religious" that they espouse the most tepid spirituality possible—and sometimes none at all. If they do bother to talk about the need to have a "relationship" with God, they conveniently lump it together with all the other "areas" of a person's life that need to be improved—like your finances or your job or your level of physical fitness.

But they've got everything backward. Of course it's important to take a holistic approach to life. As we said earlier, your body, your mind, and your spirit are all connected. But that's not the same thing as putting God on the same level as your gym membership. You can't work on spirituality the way you work on your biceps or your abs or your lower back. Your relationship with God has to inform and infuse everything you do—it has to be *over and above* everything you do.

You see, there really *is* a God and he really *does* have a plan for us. There really are such things as Good and Evil, Right and Wrong, and Objective Truth. There really is a correct map to follow. And if you trivialize these things—as the personal development industry often does—there's no chance you're ever going to experience true peace and happiness.

Well, we're not going to make the same mistake here. No matter what topics we discuss in this book, we're never going to forget the most important foundational principle of them all—we're never going to forget the answer to these three simple questions:

Where did we come from? God.
Where are we going? God.
What is life about? God.

Get that right, and everything else will be a whole lot easier—okay?
End of sermon!

PART III

Take Control

"Do what you can, with what you have, where you are."

—THEODORE ROOSEVELT

"And I tell you, ask, and it will be given to you; seek, and you will find; knock, and it will be opened to you."

—LUKE 11:9

8.

Spirituality 101

Let's take a few seconds to recap.

I've said some pretty tough things so far. I've said that most people are walking around like zombies, unaware that their priorities are completely screwed up. I've said that we need to stop whining and moaning and take ownership of our lives—especially when things aren't going right. I've said that most of us are kidding ourselves about who we really are; that we like to think we're such wonderful people when, in fact, our true, inner selves are a lot uglier than we would ever admit. I've tried hard not to pull any punches here. I've taken a real risk that all these "negative" statements might turn you off. But I've been willing to do that because I think it's a lot more important for you to wake up than it is for you to like me.

The good news is that no matter how bad things are,

there's always time to reverse course. And so I've also gone over a few basic principles that are necessary to make any kind of progress in life. I've talked about taking a mind-body-spirit approach to everything we do; I've talked about the importance of being able to about-face whenever we realize we're headed the wrong way. I've talked about the benefit of starting with small actions in order to build momentum. And finally, I've talked about the absolute necessity of putting God first—of using *his* plan and *his* map in order to be happy—not just our own self-improvement goals.

But now it's time to get into the nitty-gritty. Now it's time to take some serious action. Over the next four chapters, I'm going to give you some very specific things I'd like you to try. Small things. Simple things. Not easy things—but things that are simple to understand and to implement. And right off the bat, I want to avoid that huge error the personal development industry always seems to make—that huge error of "omission" we talked about earlier. I want to start by enlisting the help of God.

To me, what we're going to talk about now represents the basics of authentic spirituality. And I mean the *basics*.

I know that some of you might already be well advanced in the spiritual life. That's great. Maybe you'll want to skip over this part. But I wouldn't if I were you. The reason is that we're trying to do something different here. We're not only concentrating on the fundamentals—we're concentrating on doing the fundamentals *consistently* over your whole lifetime, so that your spirituality never deteriorates into a mere "phase." You don't want to be one of those spiritual "bingers," do you? You know the type—the ones who get so obsessed about God and religion, and then lose all their fervor after a while and stop completely. The aim of this book is not to form future "lapsed" Christians. It's to help you do the right thing, *all the time*.

So, to start at the beginning...

When you get up in the morning, do you know the first thing you should do? I'm talking about before you even open your eyes. I'm talking about when you're still lying there in a fog, upset that you have to get out of bed and go to work. At that very moment, just as you're starting to reenter the world of the living, you need to do one ultra-important thing. You need to say a short prayer.

Why? Because the first really conscious moment of your day should be given to God.

Now, everyone knows that prayer is the foundation of the spiritual life. There have been thousands of books written on the subject and millions of sermons preached on it. And as you get further along in the spiritual life, you'll find that there are many different ways of praying. But for our purposes, there's really no need to take something so simple and make it seem complicated. Prayer is nothing more than talking to God. It's the act of communicating with our Creator and Redeemer. Period.

In order to have a relationship with God—or with anyone, for that matter—you have to communicate, right? Communication is the key. Well, prayer opens up the communications channel with God. And it doesn't take long to do. In fact, it can almost be instantaneous. After all, how long does it take you to plug in your radio, or your computer, or your battery charger? It's the same for your morning prayer. What you need to do when you wake up is essentially "plug yourself in" to the power source of the entire universe, the power source that created the world—that created you. And the way you do that is by sending up a short message to him.

What do you say in the message? How about this: *Thank you, God, for giving me another morning. Please help me to do your will today.*

That's it! And if you really want to cover all the bases and start the day with a home run, you can say the "Our Father," too. The "Our Father"—or the "Lord's Prayer"—is the prayer that Jesus Christ himself taught. It's the prayer on which all other authentic Christian prayers are based. It contains absolutely everything you need to say to God—it praises him, thanks him, asks him for help, and asks him for forgiveness for anything you may have done wrong. Libraries of books have been written about this prayer and whole catechisms have been organized around it. It's the model for all genuine prayer.

And it's so short. Do you know how long it takes to say good morning to God, and then add an "Our Father"? Twenty-two seconds. That's right. I just timed it. And I said it very slowly, too. Can you spare twenty-two seconds every morning for the rest of your life, to the One who gave you life?

You don't think you can? You don't know if you have enough faith yet?

Listen. If you truly feel you can't say this little prayer because you don't believe in God, then all you have to do is incorporate that doubt into the prayer, itself. In other words, you can bring your lack of faith right to God's doorstep. You can say: *God, I really don't know if I believe in you yet. But if you're there, can you please increase my faith?*

Now, that's as honest and sincere as you can get. There's nothing wrong with a prayer like that. It even demonstrates a certain spirit of humility that God is sure to appreciate. But if you can't even bring yourself to do *that*, then please don't kid yourself—your problem has nothing to do with a lack of faith. It has to do with pride. I'm going to talk more about the whole "faith decision" a little later. But I'm telling you right now, an inability to even take a chance that there's a God by offering up the simplest of prayers is not a good sign that you're open to ever experiencing true happiness.

But let's say you *are* able to at least say good morning to God. That's just Step One. The next thing you have to do is go out and buy yourself a copy of the New Testament. You know the kind I mean—those small copies that can fit practically anywhere, even in your pocket? You can take them to work, or on vacation, or you can just leave them on the nightstand next to your bed. You need to go buy one. Or you need to buy one of those Bible apps for your smart-phone. There are dozens of different versions, and they're either free or very cheap! Just get one.

Why? Because you have to start reading it right away, that's why. We're talking about the Word of God. And that's something you need to hear. People all over the world whimper and whine about God's "silence." But the fact is that God talks to us in many ways. And nowhere does he speak more clearly and loudly than in Sacred Scripture.

Remember, Christians believe that Jesus Christ *is* God. He wasn't just some holy man. He wasn't just some teacher like Socrates or Confucius or Buddha. He was and is God Almighty in human form. So if you want to see God walk-ing around, you have to read the gospels. If you want to hear God speaking, you have to read the gospels. If you want to know the message that God has for the world to-day and for you, personally, you have to read the gospels.

The bottom line is that you should read a little bit of the New Testament every day. It doesn't have to be a lot. Some people read only one chapter. Some go through the whole Bible from start to finish, every year. I, myself, try to read a page or two every night. Then when I get to the end of the gospels, I start right back again at the beginning. But you don't have to be so ambitious. For now, just start with a single verse a day.

That's one little sentence! Can you handle that?

There used to be a great saying: *No Bible, no breakfast. No Bible, no bed.* In other words, you shouldn't have those eggs and bacon in the morning unless you've first nourished your soul with Scripture. You shouldn't lay your head on your pillow at night unless you've first put your day in perspective with the Word of God.

That's a wonderful rule. But for the sake of making things as easy as possible, I would say that you should *commit* to at least the second part—"No Bible, No Bed." If you have to miss the morning, fine. But you absolutely shouldn't go to sleep at night unless you've read some of your New Testament.

Is this all there is to the spiritual life? Of course not. There's much, much more. There's love of God and neighbor, there's worship, there's sacrifice, there's obedience to the Ten Commandments, there's the whole life of the church. And all of it's important. This is just the beginning. But the beginning is oh so critical: Talking to God. Reading the Scriptures. Doing it over and over again until it becomes a part of you; until saying your first prayer in the morning is as natural as taking your first breath, and as necessary; until reading the Bible at night is as automatic as brushing your teeth and putting on your pajamas.

Please don't misunderstand me. I'm not talking here about meaningless repetition or mindless rote. When you open the gospel and read that verse or that chapter, you should be listening for God to speak to you. You should have an openness to whatever God is telling you. If you're experiencing problems in your marriage or your health or your job, you have to trust that God is going to help you through your reading and your prayer. That openness and that trust and that consistency is something that God is going to reward. But you have to stick with it! You have to do it every day, no excuses.

But you're too tired, you say.

Sorry, do it anyway!

But you're sick with the flu.

Sorry, do it anyway!

But you feel like a hypocrite because you were just sinning.

Sorry, do it anyway!

None of that matters! I don't care what kinds of sins you may have committed. And I don't care if you only just committed them before sleep. Don't you go bed without praying and reading the Bible. Don't worry about "hypocrisy." Just do an about-face like we discussed a few pages ago. God will help you take care of that in his own time. You're probably not a hypocrite anyway. You're probably just a weak, habitual sinner—like the rest of us. But this is your *lifeline*. This is something that will keep you anchored to God, no matter what your emotional mood or your sinful setbacks.

So just do it! Every morning and evening without fail—starting now. And make a commitment to do it forever.

Till the day you die.

9.

Move!

Okay, you've put God first—great! That's a huge step in the right direction. You're already a million miles ahead of most of the world. But keeping in mind what we discussed earlier about taking a "full person" approach to life, what's next on the list?

The answer is simple, but once again, it's something that people either don't do enough, or do in mad binges, or do too much of—to the point where it becomes almost a kind of religion of its own. I'm talking about taking care of your body. In particular I'm talking about exercise.

Let's start with the people who do too much. There *is* such a thing as focusing too much on your health. G. K. Chesterton said that the mere "pursuit of health" for health's sake "always leads to something unhealthy. Physical nature must be enjoyed, not worshipped."

The folks who spend three hours at the gym every day, who eat nothing but organic fruit and nuts, and whose biggest holiday of the year is Earth Day have obviously crossed a line. Their main problem—though they don't know it—is a moral one. They're essentially doing what Chesterton warned against: worshipping nature, specifically their own bodies. For them, health has become an "idol"—their highest goal and aspiration in life.

Only it's not supposed to be the highest goal. Health is a secondary goal. It's only a means to an end, and not the end itself. The true "end" or "purpose" of life is to be in union with God; to do his will—thereby ensuring not only eternal life in heaven, but also peace and happiness right now.

That's the ultimate objective of life. Not good health, not longevity, not the preservation of youth. And so these people who obsess over their bodies and nature to an inordinate degree have themselves become "unnatural." Their priorities are all wrong—and so they usually end up being wrong on a slew of other moral issues as well.

But let's put these people aside for the moment. Let's say that you've got your priorities right. Let's say your problem isn't that you're fixated on your body, but rather the opposite—that you're like most people in society who neglect their bodies. Maybe you *really* neglect it. Did you know that's immoral, too?

Of course it is. The body is the temple of the Holy

Spirit, remember? That's straight from the Bible. And doesn't it make sense? If the goal of life is to perform God's will, then won't you be able to do that in a more vibrant and perfect way if you have good health? Doesn't it follow logically that if you take care of your body you'll also have more energy and more mobility and more strength and may even be able to live longer? Won't you therefore be able to do what God wants you to do in the most efficient, effective way possible?

That's just common sense. The Eastern religions don't have any monopoly on the "spirituality of health." On the contrary, it's the very essence of Christianity to be active, energetic, exuberant, and above all—on the move. Christianity is a religion not only of great emotion—but also of great *motion*. From the very beginning, it's been marching, moving, spreading, and running.

Just read the gospel accounts of the Resurrection of Christ. You'll see women running from the empty tomb to find the disciples; you'll see Mary Magdalene running to give Peter the news that she saw the risen Christ; you'll see Peter and John running back in excitement, almost racing to see who would get there first. There's just a lot of running going on. In fact, the end of the gospels is filled with physical movement. Peter even dives into the water and swims to the shore like an Olympic athlete when he recognizes Jesus standing there.

And that's not the end of it. After Christ commands the apostles to go into the whole world and spread the good news, a period of feverish activity begins. The letters of St. Paul contain an abundant number of words and phrases having to do with athletic competition—"boxing," "strenuous exercise," "striving for mastery," "running a race with perseverance," "winning," to name just a few. In his second letter to Timothy he famously writes: "I have fought the good fight, I have finished the race, I have kept the faith."

None of these metaphors is an accident. The whole point of Christianity is to advance, to be on the march. When you have good news, the last thing you want to do is sit down and keep it to yourself. Rather, you want to share it with everyone. Especially *this* good news. The message of the gospels is that death is *not* the end of life, that suffering is *not* the end of the story, that there *is* a God, that he *does* love us, and that we're going to live forever in heaven if we embrace that truth with faith. That's not the kind of information you keep secret.

Even the main symbol of Christianity is a metaphor for action. Look at the cross and compare it to the traditional symbols of Eastern religions like Buddhism—which are always circular in design. Eastern religions are all about looking inward, meditating on oneself or about the infinite circle of life. Christianity, on the other hand, is all about dynamic movement, and so its symbol is made up of two bold, crossed lines extending outward to all points of the globe—north, south, east, and west. Ultimately, Christianity is a faith of joyful action, and if you believe in it and want to spread it, it's important that you, yourself, are able to take action with energy and decisiveness.

Now, let me take a second to clarify something. I know there are people out there who are elderly and sick and unable to get around. I've just pointed out the connection between Christianity and motion, but I don't want anyone to get the wrong idea. No matter what stage of life you're at, no matter how sick or handicapped you are, you can *always* do God's will. Even if you're stuck on a hospital bed with all kinds of tubes coming out of you, you can still be a shining example to others of how to face suffering with courage and faith. And like the battery of a car, which doesn't move at all but which gives power to the entire vehicle, you can be motionless yourself and still move the whole world through the power of your prayers. Every human being, from conception till natural death, has more dignity than a billion soulless galaxies. A person's worth is not decreased one iota because he or she can't move. That's been a bedrock belief of Christianity for two thousand years.

But I'm not talking about that here. I'm assuming that you're *not* at death's door. I'm assuming that even if you're old and sick, you still have some energy left in your body—

some ability to move. And if that's the case, then everything I'm saying applies to you. We all know how important movement is. In fact, there's not a health book or program in the world that doesn't insist on the need for weekly aerobic activity. It's just essential for your physical well-being— and your mental and emotional well-being as well.

That's one of the reasons people today are so unhappy. So many of us live sedentary lives. We get up in the morning and sit in our cars on the way to work, then we sit at our desks for eight hours, then we drive back home and sit at our dinner tables to eat, then we sit in front of the TV or computer and play video games or fool around with social media, then we finally go to bed and lie there for another eight hours before getting up and starting the whole process over again. And we do this every week for years on end. Then we wonder why we've got the energy, physique, and emotional outlook of a slug-worm!

Look, I'm no doctor, but I'll tell you something now that's as true as anything you'll ever read in a health magazine or psychology journal. If you want your life to change for the better, you've got to get *moving*. Regular movement improves everything. Your energy levels. Your stress levels. Your ability to sleep. Your ability to digest. Your breathing. Your body weight. Your blood pressure. Your circulation. It causes your body to release powerful chemicals called endorphins, which make you feel more relaxed and elated, and also make your immune system more resistant to sickness and disease. It helps your body to quickly change emotional states in ways we don't fully understand. Sometimes just shaking your whole body out and briskly walking around the block or jogging in place can do wonders for relieving the daily doldrums or even more serious problems with depression.

There's just no way around it. You've got to move, move, move, and you've got to keep moving. In fact, when you stop moving completely, that's when you know you're dead! The good news is that this isn't hard. This isn't about training for an Olympic decathlon or subjecting your body to great stress. Do you know how much exercise is required for optimal health? *Three or four days a week for thirty to sixty minutes at a time.* That's it! And it makes no difference what kind of movement it is—running, walking, swimming, cycling, general aerobics work—all of it is good. Nor should the exercise be too strenuous. The purpose of those thirty minutes is just to get your heart rate up and to keep it up. In fact, you should be able to carry on a normal conversation as you're moving without having to catch your breath. If you can't do that, then you're going too fast.

Remember, we're not talking about a weight-loss plan here. We're not talking about a fitness program. We're talking about a simple thing you can do to significantly improve your physical, mental, and emotional health, *immediately.*

Do you know that if you exercised for thirty minutes, three times a week, and did it consistently for a decade, you'd be much healthier, overall, than ninety percent of the people who take vitamins and minerals and herbs and aromatherapy and who binge on exercise fads and crazy diets, but then stop after a few years because of injuries or emotional problems or family problems or a thousand other things?

The key is consistency. This whole book is really about consistency—doing the simplest, most basic things, but doing them over and over until they become part of who you are. Sure, it's easy to get motivated by something you read or hear and then go to the gym a few times. But it's quite another thing to find a way to consistently exercise even when the weather is bad, or when you're feeling depressed, or when you can't pay your bills, or when the kids are screaming, or when you feel like it's a waste of time because you've been eating so badly. That's when you really find out what you're made of.

You really have to approach this problem as if it's a military campaign. You have to look at your week with a cold, objective eye and ask yourself a whole series of questions. Where can you find three thirty-minute blocks? How can you carve out the time, given all the other obligations in your life? Do you have any health-conscious friends you can make plans with? Are there any outdoor sports you can take up? Do you have a dog you can walk? Is there a playground you can take him to? If you're able to afford a gym membership, how are you going to deal with the boredom of jogging or walking or biking on an exercise machine? Can you listen to audio books or music? Can you spend the time praying?

In other words, you really have to think about how you're going to tackle this. You have to find a way to make this time not only doable but *enjoyable*. Remember, this isn't just about your body. It's about your whole being. More important, it's about your relationship with God and your ability to do what he wants you to do more perfectly and effectively. If you're healthier, he's going to utilize you to help him in a greater variety of ways. That's serious business—a lot more serious than just trying to lose a few pounds, don't you agree?

The bottom line is this: If you're not feeling particularly good about your life—or if you're just feeling a little sluggish or sad—try to snap out of it for a second. Stop thinking all those hopeless thoughts! Remember that motion and emotion are intimately connected. Take a break and go outside. Walk around the block. Try to figure out how you're going to execute the simple plan I've suggested here—and how you're going to stick to it.

In other words, try taking a lesson from the early Christians. Get off your rear and *move*!

10.

Bringing Order Out of Chaos

Here's another spiritual principle that has far-ranging implications—especially in terms of helping us to take control of our lives. From the beginning of the Bible to the end, one thing is extraordinarily clear: *God is a God of Order*.

The very first thing God did after he created the universe was to organize the universe—to separate light from darkness, to divide the water and the land, to bring clarity to the chaos. Now, of course these images aren't scientific. They aren't meant to be. Sacred Scripture should never be confused with a high school physics textbook. The point of Scripture is to present the deeper, underlying truth about life. And the tremendous truth being conveyed in the opening pages of the book of Genesis has to do with the nature of God.

God is simple in substance. God is Purity. God is Order. That's the truth to get into our heads.

And when God became Man in the person of Jesus Christ, he demonstrated those same characteristics again. Christ came into the world to perform a certain mission—the salvation of humanity. And he did it with extraordinary speed, order, and effectiveness. He was born in a very simple manner and then spent the first thirty years of his life in total, hidden quiet, preparing himself. Once he began, it took him only three short years to accomplish his objective. In three years he turned the whole world upside down—and it hasn't been the same since. Three years! That's efficiency for you! That's God.

When Christ died on the cross and rose from the dead, he did something else that showed this characteristic. On that first Easter Sunday morning, when the apostles discovered his empty tomb, they noticed something very interesting. They noticed that the burial shroud that had been used to cover Jesus' face was rolled up neatly in the corner. Such a tiny detail. But what significance! It means that when Jesus Christ rose from the dead, the first thing he did was to tidy up! The first thing he did was to put everything in its proper place—to clean his tomb before leaving it forever.

And of course, that's to be expected. After all, Christ is God. And God's nature is to be orderly and clean.

What we've got to keep in mind here is that the thing most contrary to God is *sin*. The act of sinning is simply the act of turning away from God, right? Well, when we turn away from God—and then move in the opposite direction—what invariably happens is that we begin to take on qualities that are *different* than God; qualities that are *contrary* to God; qualities that are *opposite* to God. And that includes disorder.

Sin, in its very nature, is division. It's disintegration. It's a falling apart—a breakdown of order. When we're not acting in line with God's will for us, that kind of disintegration happens to us on the inside—in our soul. There's an internal collapse that's not immediately perceptible to the people around us; an invisible chaos that we're sometimes not even aware of, even though we usually *feel* it in the form of unhappiness.

The good news is that what happens to us on the inside is sure to turn up on the outside—if we give it enough time. In other words, when our internal lives are messy, our exterior lives eventually become messy, too. I say this is good news because if there's a visible manifestation of the internal chaos, at least it can be a sign to us that something needs to change.

What happens when things break down morally and spiritually for us is that our *whole life* breaks down as well. And I mean this in the most literal way. It's not just that our relationships break down or our finances break down—though these things certainly can occur. I mean that our homes and our offices and our cars break down, too. They all get sloppy. They all get dirty. Disorder prevails. Chaos reigns.

And this is the point we need to understand. When we finally become tired of the chaos and emotional turmoil that often accompany a spiritual breakdown, it's almost instinctive for us to want to physically clean up. No matter what the root problem is, we know deep down that we have to start eliminating the clutter. And so it's common to hear people say they've had enough and are finally going to force themselves to clean their closet or their garage or whatever.

Sometimes people will poke fun at this natural inclination. They'll say that it's mere avoidance; that it's like "putting a Band-Aid on cancer." That because we don't want to take on the more painful, deeper problems in our marriage and our job and our finances; we instead tend to work on other less challenging tasks, like cleaning the closet. We do this, they say, in order to fool ourselves into believing that we're really making progress, to *distract* ourselves from the main problems of life, to simply make ourselves "feel good." In other words, some people think we're just wasting our time by cleaning up.

But guess what? They're wrong! They're missing the point completely. They're missing the whole spiritual significance of disorder. And so naturally they end up in a muddle, themselves.

Sure, if cleaning up were the only thing a person ever did to combat his or her problems, it would qualify as a distraction. But it's not meant to be the only thing. It's meant to be a step. A step in the right direction. A step to build momentum. And we've already talked about how important momentum is.

Straightening up and putting things in order is always a good thing to do. The reason is that it's a sign you're trying to be in union with God—who, as we said, *is* order. No matter the problem, cleaning your desk or your office or your house is necessary because it's an attempt to make your work and living space more "God-like." It's an attempt to conform these spaces to God's nature. And that's never a mistake.

The same goes for cleaning yourself. Have you ever noticed that when things start to go really wrong in your life, all you want to do is stay in bed? When you're feeling lousy, it's difficult to even get washed and dressed and groomed in the morning. In addition to the other problems you have, there always seems to be an extra temptation to indulge in the sin of sloth—better known as laziness—especially with regard to your appearance and your schedule. Why do you think that is?

I'll tell you the answer—and I know I keep hammering

home this same point—but *everything is connected.* The body, mind, and spirit are all tied together. What you do to one affects the other two—and the whole. If you're moving toward God, that is, trying to do *his* will, play by *his* rules, follow *his* map, then everything else in your life will start to "align" itself, too, eventually resulting in greater peace and happiness. If you're moving away from God, that is, trying to do *your* will, play by *your* rules, and follow *your* map, then everything else in your life will start to get chaotic and confused, not to mention depressing. And that's going to result in lethargy.

One of the best ways to combat this deterioration is to systematically eliminate the chaos from your life. You've heard the old saying, "Cleanliness is next to godliness"? Well, it's truer that you ever imagined. In fact, it's one of the most important spiritual truths in the universe. And it's time we all tried to make it part of our lifestyle.

But hold on, you say. This doesn't make sense. There are plenty of Hollywood movie stars, rock stars, and billionaires who are living morally bankrupt lives, but who seem to be quite content and quite organized. They flaunt their bad behavior publicly, and bash Christianity every chance they get, and yet they always look so beautiful and pristine and fashionable. Surely their lives are orderly. Surely they're happy. But how can that be? Have these folks managed to find some loophole in the spiritual law?

No, they haven't! The truth is that they may seem happy, but they're not. Don't believe it! If you look past the glamour and glitz and thick makeup, you'll quickly see all the tangled confusion of their lives—all the broken marriages, all the lawsuits, all the divided property, all the scattered children, all the tax problems, all the drug and alcohol problems, all the overdoses, all the infidelities, all the depression, all the suicides, all the *mess*.

None of it is clean and orderly. None of it is truly joyful. Remember what Christ said about the Pharisees. He called them "whitewashed tombs, which on the outside appear beautiful, but on the inside are full of dead men's bones and all uncleanness."

You can't allow that to be you. This book is not about becoming "whitewashed tombs." You may be a weak and sinful human being, but you at least have to try to do God's will. You at least have to try to be "clean"—on the inside *and* the outside. That's what makes all the difference.

So here's the bottom line: You need to take a quick survey of your life and then make a list of all the areas that need to be straightened out. Then you need to start cleaning up—one mess at a time. First your desk, then your office, then your emails, then your computer files, then your kitchen, then your garage, then your vehicle, then your closets, then your clothes. In whatever order you prefer. I know this can be a challenge—especially if you have young kids running around the house leaving havoc in their wake. But you have to try!

And if you happen to be depressed, you have to force yourself to take that extra-long shower in the morning. You have to make an effort to dress nicely. Not fancy. Not expensive. You don't need to wear Armani suits or Ferragamo shoes. This isn't about being extravagant. It's about being clean and neat and well put together—no matter what your emotional or physical condition.

Then you need to try to clean up your head. Your mind can get more cluttered than any room in your home because there are an infinite number of things you can put there. Did you ever see one of those computer screens that have hundreds of different windows opened at the same time? Doesn't your brain feel like that sometimes? Well, it's time to start closing those windows and shutting down those open programs. Do you know how to do that? By focusing. By taking some quiet time every day and concentrating on God. The secular world calls it meditation. But Christians call it prayer.

Please don't get stressed over any of this. There's no need to do everything at once. I don't care if I sound like a broken record, but slow and steady wins the race. What we're interested in here is long-lasting change—not a mere spring cleaning. Little by little, start to bring your life under the sovereignty of God's Order.

Then just watch the results. Within a few weeks time, you'll see an amazing transformation take place. I guarantee that as all the clutter begins to clear, the path leading to true peace and happiness will become a whole lot easier for you to see—and to follow.

11.

Controlling Your Rudder

I'd like you to try an experiment. Open your left hand right now and examine your palm. Look at the line going in a zigzag pattern, up and down, up and down. Can you see the M shape formed by the creases in your skin? Sometimes it's a little difficult to make out, but it's there. Everyone has it. Now do the same with your right hand. With your palm open, can you see the M there, right in the middle?

Do you know what the old mystics used to do—the old hermits and monks of the Middle Ages? Every morning, before they began their day, they would look at their two outstretched palms—at the two M's carved into their hands—and they would meditate on the Latin words, *Memento Mori*: "Remember you will die!"

Do you think that's morbid? I don't. I call that perspective. I call that wisdom. Let's be honest. No matter how fit you are or how good your genetics, nobody has any guarantee of longevity. You can be the healthiest person in the world and you can still get hit by a bus. It's impossible to say enough times, but the same God who gave you the morning doesn't promise you the evening. If there was one truth I could drill into people's heads, it would be that. Not because I'm cynical or fatalistic. Quite the contrary; I try to be upbeat about everything. But that's not the same as denying reality. To be a Christian doesn't mean you check your brains at the door. God gave us those brains for a reason. To use them. To recognize and accept certain facts. And the fact is, you can die at *any* time. Therefore you have to be prepared at *all* times. Nobody gets out of this life alive. So you always have to have your bags packed. You always have to be in a state of mental, emotional, and spiritual *readiness*. That's not being cynical—it's being intelligent.

Now does that mean you have to live in fear? Of course not! All I'm saying is that you can't afford to blindly waste years on activities that get you nowhere and don't add one iota to your real happiness. And that's what people do all the time. They just waste whole decades. Then they get old or sick, and finally, when they see that the end is in sight, *then* they start spending more time on matters of real consequence—on spiritual matters, moral matters, matters having to do with their eternal soul.

Which is why I want to give you a shortcut now. A way

to save time, or make up for time that's already been lost. What I'm about to tell you is very important and I don't want you to think I'm exaggerating for the sake of effect. You won't read it in most self-improvement books or even spiritual books. And yet, if you put this shortcut into practice, I can practically guarantee you that you'll eliminate eighty percent of your emotional and spiritual problems—and probably most of your other faults as well. That's a big promise, I know. But it's true. It has to do with the way we communicate.

St. James, who was an Apostle of Christ and one of his closest friends, made the following statement in a famous epistle he wrote:

Any man among you who is perfect in speech,
is a perfect man.

The profound shortcut that God has to offer you is this: if you guard your speech closely and somehow manage to control your tongue, you will consequently control everything else in your life. *Everything*.

What you've got to understand is that the tongue is exactly like the rudder of a ship. You know what the rudder does? It steers the ship; it controls the ship. Now, compared to the size of a ship itself, the rudder is very small. In fact you can't even see it because it's underwater. And yet, when it moves in a certain direction, the whole ship obeys its command and moves with it. It doesn't matter how fierce the winds may be or how high the seas are or how much power is being exerted by the engines; the ship goes wherever that little rudder tells it to go.

Well, that's the same effect the tongue has on the human person. It's our rudder. It's what steers us. It may be small and unseen, but the power it has over what we do and how we act and where we go is incredible. Control the rudder, control the ship. Tame your tongue, tame yourself. It's that simple.

Unfortunately, the reverse is also true. If you fail to control your tongue, you become just like a ship with a broken rudder. You drift aimlessly—or even worse, you crash into other ships or into the dock or the shore. People who don't discipline their tongues go through life destroying everything in their wake. Eventually they become shipwrecked themselves, and sink into a sea of their own misery—misery brought about because of the way they've managed to alienate everyone around them.

You know this is true! How many things have you said in your life that you wish you could take back now? Especially all those stupid things said in anger. I can tell you from my own experience that there are things I said thirty years ago that literally make me cringe when I recall them now. Three decades ago—and they still cause me pain!

Human beings have learned to conquer all kinds of harsh environments on the earth and under the sea and even in outer space—but we can't seem to conquer our own tongues. Why?

It goes back again to perspective. Most people today who have poisonous tongues—tongues that spread anger and rumors and gossip and scandal and lies—have completely lost sight of perspective. They spend their lives "majoring in the minors," and, as Richard Carlson said in his bestselling book, "sweating the small stuff."

Those medieval mystics were right. In fact, they had another great Latin saying: *Quid Hoc Ad Aeternitatem.* "What is this in light of eternity?" In other words, why do we get so angry and upset about our problems, when nothing really matters in comparison to the "big picture"—the picture that involves death and judgment and heaven and hell?

We see a little child in a department store crying because his father won't buy him a certain toy. He's moaning and screaming, all because he's not getting what he wants. At that moment, he's really experiencing a tragedy. He's dying inside because he isn't getting that toy. The other people in the store might be amused at the scene and even laugh. Why? Because they know how unimportant that toy really is. They've lived a little. They have mortgages. They have marriages. They have bills. They have people in their lives whom they've loved and lost. They know what real tragedy is. And they laugh to see a child throwing a temper tantrum over something as meaningless as a toy. In other words, they've gained some perspective.

Well, guess what? The saints in heaven are laughing at us! We throw temper tantrums all the time because we don't get what we want. Our spouses don't give us the support we need; our children don't give us the appreciation we deserve; our boss doesn't give us the pay raise we've earned, the clerk behind the counter doesn't give us the respect we're due.

They're not giving us the toys we want! Yes, in the light of eternity those things are all just toys.

You don't think so? One day you might. One day (heaven forbid), when you come out of the doctor's office and you've just been given the news that the tumor they found is malignant and nothing more can be done, and you walk onto the sunny street and see a cabdriver screaming expletives at the car in front of him for not moving fast enough, and a child crying because his ice-cream cone has fallen on the sidewalk, and a woman yelling at her husband for God-knows-what-reason—then you're going to understand what true perspective is. Then you're going to understand why deeply spiritual people of every generation and every faith tradition have always seemed so calm and quiet and free from anxiety. It's because they know the answer to the question: *What is this in light of eternity?*

But then again, maybe you're one of those fortunate people who are serene by nature—who would never think of uttering a nasty word. I envy you! I happen to be from New York City. I don't like stereotypes, but I have to admit, some of us here have a tendency to express our emotions in ways that are a bit unproductive and uncharitable. We have difficulty with our volume control. We understand the challenge of keeping calm.

But maybe you're not like that. Maybe you have the disposition of an angel. Maybe you're a soft-spoken midwesterner. Or a friendly southerner. Or a strong but silent Texan. Or a polite and proper Englishman—I'm really letting the stereotypes fly now! Does that mean this "shortcut" won't work for you?

Not at all. Because I guarantee you *still* have a problem with your tongue. Controlling your speech isn't just about anger management. There's a lot more to it. For instance...

Do you ever lie?

Do you ever brag?

Do you ever complain?

Do you ever gossip?

Do you ever ridicule others?

Do you ever rashly judge people?

Do you ever use silent body language to convey your
anger, or sarcastic "tones" of voice?

Come on, be honest! You know you do. We *all* do.

Guarding our speech and controlling our tongue isn't
just about the nasty things we say. It's about all the garbage
that comes out of our mouths on a daily basis. Christ was
very clear about the matter. He told his disciples, "When
you have to say yes, say yes; when you have to say no, say
no. Anything else is from the evil one." What could be simpler to understand?

I'm not claiming it's easy to be perfect in your speech.
It's not. Shortcuts can be difficult—brutally difficult. But
that's why this one works. Christ said at another time that
what "defiles" a person is not what goes into his body,
but rather what "comes out of his mouth"—because what
comes out of the mouth really originates in the heart. That's
the true source of all our pride and greed and jealousy and
lust and gluttony and laziness and anger.

Therefore, if we somehow manage to stop the outpour-
ing of filth, we're bound to see a change in our lives. If
we have the kind of strength it takes to control the "exit
point" for all our verbal toxins, we're going to also be vic-
torious over all our other sins as well—including the secret
ones we never utter a word about. That's why St. James

said, "Any man among you who is perfect in speech, is a perfect man."

So, yes, it's going to be hard. But luckily this book isn't about instantaneous success. It's about building momentum. It's about getting on the right road to peace and happiness and staying there. Like everything else we've talked about, we're going to move forward a little bit at a time.

With that in mind, if you're the type of person who curses frequently, then for the next few days you should try eliminating all expletives from your speech. No more obscenities. No more vulgarities. No more excuses. Just stop cold. If you're the type of person who doesn't have a problem with profanity, then try something else. Pick two or three of the other "imperfections" listed above and eliminate those from your speech. Stop gossiping for once in your life! Stop bragging! Stop complaining!

Do your best to discipline yourself—at least for the remainder of the time it takes to finish this book. And then, if you like the transformation that occurs, by all means continue the process. Ultimately, the goal here isn't just to clean up your speech. It's to clean up your soul. If you tame your tongue, you tame yourself. If you conquer your mouth, then you conquer your life.

And if you experience any setbacks along the way—as you certainly will—just keep reminding yourself of the importance of perspective. Keep thinking of those ancient mystics and their wise old sayings:

Memento Mori!—Remember you will die!
Quid Hoc Ad Aeternitatem?—What is this in light of eternity?

PART IV

Decide

"Take the first step in faith. You don't have to see the whole staircase, just take the first step."
—Dr. Martin Luther King, Jr.

"Therefore everyone who hears these words of mine and puts them into practice is like a wise man who built his house on the rock. The rain came down, the streams rose, and the winds blew and beat against that house; yet it did not fall, because it had its foundation on the rock."
—Matthew 7: 24–26

12.

Time to Get off the Fence

Hopefully you've been building some momentum and laying the groundwork for what might become an important transformation in your life. If you have, that's great. I would love to shake your hand because you're already way ahead of most people in this world. But now we're about to enter a new phase. We've come to a point where we really need to make a few decisions.

Every decision you make in life—even the smallest—has the potential to be important, because every decision starts you down a pathway. Take another example from aviation. You know that a jet can depart from New York and fly toward Rome, but if it changes course so much as a few degrees at the beginning, its flight path will be altered by hundreds of miles. By the time the plane gets across the ocean, it will actually be headed to a completely different city—maybe even a completely different continent.

That's the way it is in life sometimes. It's possible for you to make a very quiet decision—a decision no one else knows about—and yet change everything. It might take years for the difference to become noticeable. But in reality, the whole flight path of your existence has been altered.

That's happened to me a couple of times. I remember once when I was in my mid-twenties, I was sitting down at the family table having lunch. It was just a normal summer Sunday, and I was munching on a sandwich and reading the newspaper. The TV was on in the background and my mother and father and brothers were all hanging around, talking. Suddenly my younger sister walked through the door and casually threw a plastic bag on the table that contained a few crosses. She said that someone she knew at church had given them to her, and that if I wanted, I could take one.

Now, at the time I wasn't a serious Christian at all. I never prayed or read the Bible or tried to obey any of the commandments. In fact, I couldn't name the commandments if you asked me. Sure, there had been times when I thought about God and wondered whether or not I really believed in him; and of course at Christmas and Easter I occasionally went to church. But all I was really interested in were girls. God was absolutely nowhere on my radar screen. And yet, for some unknown reason, on that lazy, ordinary summer afternoon, I found myself staring at that bag of crosses.

I had never liked wearing jewelry, but I decided I would try one on—just to see what it was like. After all, I spent a lot of time going to the beach, and it might look "cool" to wear something around my neck. So I found the plainest cross in the bag—one that wasn't fancy or expensive at all, just simple stainless steel—and put it on.

And then something interesting happened. Just at the moment I clasped the chain around my neck, a very quiet but very clear thought occurred to me: *Does this mean I'm a Christian?*

At that point in my life, I knew very little about Christianity. I certainly didn't have any kind of "relationship" with Christ. So I asked myself the question: Do I want to just wear this cross for no reason—or do I perhaps want to find out more about what it means? Without really thinking, I made a decision. I would keep the cross on for a little while to see if I liked it, and at the same time I would try to pick up a book during the week to at least refresh myself on the basics of Christianity.

All of this happened in my mind very quickly. The newspaper and half-eaten sandwich were still in front of me. The TV was on and my family was talking in the background. I went right back to eating lunch. On the surface it seemed as if nothing had happened. And yet something monumental had happened. I had made a decision that put me on a very specific path, a path that would lead me—over the course of several decades—on a great adventure, an adventure that has ultimately culminated in you reading these words right now.

Do you see what I'm trying to get at? The power of decisions can never be underestimated! Even the tiniest ones can change your life forever. That's why we need to start discussing them now. In fact there are three in particular we need to focus on. And the first of these is the most critical.

We've talked a little in this book about God. But now it's time to get serious about him. Now it's time to make a genuine decision about faith.

So many people mistakenly think that faith is a feeling. It's not. It's a decision. Feelings are mushy. Feelings are inconsistent. Feelings go up and down. One day you feel depressed; the next day you feel elated. One moment you feel that everything is black and cloudy. The next moment you feel a glimmer of hope and everything is sunshine. Sometimes what you eat makes you feel a certain way. Sometimes the weather makes you feel a certain way. Sometimes the music you hear makes you feel a certain way. Sometimes a particular person or place or occasion makes you feel a certain way. Sometimes you know why you feel the way you do; sometimes you have no clue. Feelings can be joyous or exhilarating or passionate or hateful or dull or depressing—but the one thing they never seem to be is predictable.

Personal development experts love to talk about the ability we have to change our feelings; to do things that make us feel confident, motivated, empowered, etc. And they're right. We *can* change them. We're *not* slaves to them. But it takes work to alter our emotions—hard work. There's a certain moral and emotional "gravity" that's always trying to pull us down, to keep us from being on an even keel. In fact there's a theological reason for this that goes back to the Garden of Eden and our fallen human nature. We'll talk more about that later. But the point is that no matter how successful we are at controlling our feelings, we're always going to be on an emotional roller coaster to some extent. And we just can't afford to base the most important decisions of our life on what amounts to a ride.

Let's be honest. Sometimes it's easy to *feel* that God exists and that he loves us. Other times—especially when someone we love dies—it's easy to feel that he's silent or nonexistent. I've got news for you: Even if you were the holiest person in the world and had the most fervent faith, there still might be times when you'd feel like an agnostic or even an atheist. Does that surprise you? It shouldn't. Some of the most famous saints in history have gone through periods of profound spiritual darkness, periods when they didn't have any strong emotional feelings about God, when they felt totally "dry." Did that prevent them from being holy? Did it prevent them from having faith? Not one bit. Their feelings may have wavered, but their faith never did. I can't emphasize this enough: The world of faith and the world of feelings are two entirely different things, and sometimes they exist on two entirely different planes.

Even if you were to witness a bona fide miracle, it still wouldn't "prove" that God exists. God himself has told us this. He's made it abundantly clear that faith is a *test*—not a demonstration. And if you've spent any time at all in school, you know that while a test is in progress, the teacher is usually silent. So if you're waiting around to see some great blazing cross appear in the sky, you're going to be waiting a long time. God just isn't going to show himself to us in bodily form. He isn't going to materialize and start performing miracles and raising people from the dead. He did that once before—and was crucified.

No. God has said time and again that we have to believe in him *without* the benefit of seeing with our eyes. He's given us all the information we need—all the evidence of nature and logic and common sense and reliable testimonies and revelation—but he's left it to us to make the final decision, despite how our feelings might fluctuate.

And don't think that atheists have any kind of free pass when it comes to emotional highs and lows, either. They don't. If you've been struggling with faith, your doubts aren't going to magically disappear if you decide to "throw in the towel" and become an unbeliever. There are still going to be moments when you have the feeling that God *does* exist. There will still be quiet, eerie nights when you gaze up at the vast array of stars sparkling in the heavens and feel deep down that there *has to be* some Being that created it all. There will still be times when you hear a powerful piece of music or see a beautiful painting or read a deeply moving passage of literature, and your soul stirs inside you and whispers that there *must* be some grand cosmic artist behind it all. There will still be moments when you're in the midst of great suffering, and out of nowhere, a friend or a stranger does something so kind for you, so compassionate, so *good*, that you actually break down in tears and feel that there must be such a thing as the human *spirit*—a spirit made in the image and likeness of goodness itself.

The bottom line is that the atheist position is just too full of holes for anyone to really feel certain about it. I've discussed this before in other books, but it's worth repeating. Atheists are always claiming that it's "superstitious" to believe in God. But the exact opposite is true. There are dozens of logical arguments for God's existence. It's atheism that's founded on a superstition—a superstition that says that life has no meaning.

We *know* life has meaning—it's preposterous to deny it. Just think about it for a moment. Atheists want us to believe that the world is made up of *physical objects* and nothing else. They want us to believe that everything in life—our thoughts, our dreams, our passions, our loves, our hates, our hopes, our virtues, our sins, our griefs, our guilts, our philosophies, our arts, our politics, our literature, our music, our history, our deepest desire for God and love and Eternal Life—that *all* of this is purely the result of bio-chemical reactions and the random movement of atoms!

That's not logic. That's superstition!

And that's why the truly great geniuses in history (including people like Albert Einstein) were never stone-cold atheists. They all knew there had to be something else in life besides physical matter. They all recognized the fact that the deeper you go into the sciences, the more mysterious the universe actually is.

There's simply no scientific answer to the question "Where did everything come from?" There's no scientific answer to the question "How can matter be eternal?" There's no scientific answer to the question "How can something come from nothing?" There's no scientific answer to the question "Why is the universe so organized?" There's no scientific answer to the question "How did life arise from lifelessness?"

Scientists don't have the answer to any of these questions—and they never will. So if you think atheism is the solution to your doubts, you've been misinformed.

That road just leads to more uncertainties and more riddles. The fact is that nothing you do or read is ever going to give you anything resembling a mathematical proof either that God exists or that he doesn't exist. It always comes back to the necessity of making a choice. You must make a choice.

And I mean *must*. That's the point so many people miss. They think they can just sail through life without making a real decision about God and it won't cost them anything. What self-delusion! We've been so brainwashed into believing that the greatest thing in the world to have is an "open mind," and that the greatest thing to do is "search" for answers. But that's nonsense. The whole point of searching for something is to eventually find it. The whole point of having an open mind is so that it can eventually close—on the truth! An open mind is not an amorphous mind. A worthwhile search is not an endless, hopeless one. Don't believe the lies of the world. If you're past twenty-five years old and haven't made a definitive decision about God, then you've got your priorities misaligned. You can't afford to waste any more time. It's time to get off the fence!

Look, making a decision doesn't just involve assessing all the facts. It involves assessing all the *risks*. And there are huge risks associated with rejecting God. You may not be aware of them because the world never talks about them.

But the fact is, you're called to a *greatness* the world knows nothing about. You're called to a *peace* the world knows nothing about. You're called to a *love* the world knows nothing about. You're called to a supernatural end—*heaven*—the world knows nothing about. All those things result from having a relationship with God. When you cut God off, you cut them off, too.

Let's say I gave you a key to an old storage unit I owned and said you could keep whatever was inside—maybe some pieces of furniture worth a few hundred dollars. You might take the key or you might not, depending on your situation. But what if I were Donald Trump and gave you a key to my personal storage vault in Atlantic City? What if I told you that I wasn't quite sure, but there *might* be a cash box there with a million dollars inside? Would you take the key from me then? I bet you would. I bet you wouldn't be able to grab it from my hands fast enough. And it wouldn't matter one bit whether you were sure there was money inside— the *possibility* would just be too great to pass by.

Or let's say you notice a stray wire coming out of some battery-operated device in your kitchen. It wouldn't be any big deal if you touched it, right? Even if the device were turned on, the electric current just wouldn't be that strong. The most you'd get from touching it is a little shock. But what if a 20,000-volt cable were placed in front of you? Would you take a chance grabbing hold of that? Would it matter much if you didn't know if the electricity was on or off? Of course not! You'd be crazy to take *any* kind of chance with it.

Are you getting what I'm saying here? When it comes to deciding whether or not to have faith, the risk-reward ratio is all in God's favor. That's not meant to scare you. It's just the plain truth. If you choose to deny God, you stand to lose everything. If you choose to believe in him, you stand to gain everything.

It's up to you to decide which it's going to be. And it doesn't matter one bit how you feel. Remember the story in the gospels about the man who begged Jesus to heal his son? The boy had been suffering from some kind of demonic illness since childhood and no one could cure him. But Jesus assured him, "If you believe, all things are possible." To which the father responded: *"Lord, I believe. Help my unbelief."*

That really captures everything I've been trying to say here. Without hesitating, the father declared his *decision*: "I believe." But he followed it up immediately with an emotional plea: "Help my unbelief." What he was basically saying was that despite his free-will choice, there was still a part of him that didn't *feel* faith.

But what did Jesus do? Did he criticize the man? Did he tell him he had to have *more* faith? No! He immediately reached out and healed the man's son. In other words, the man's decision to believe was enough. It was all Christ required to grant his request and show him the healing power of God.

The same goes for you and me. I said before that even if you decide to believe, your feelings might sometimes waver—especially during periods of grief or tragedy. But I wasn't quite giving you the whole story. I didn't say that after you make your faith decision, something else will happen, too. In the deepest part of your being—the part made in the image and likeness of God—a different kind of certitude will begin to form. Only this certitude won't be based on feelings, but on grace—a gift of divine help from God, himself. And once this faith takes hold, it will grow, and grow, and grow until it literally transforms every aspect of your life. It will take away your fear. It will take away your loneliness. It will take away your despair. It will give you a whole new perspective—a perspective that transcends all emotions and all feelings and all circumstances. You see, when you get to *know* God, instead of just knowing *about* him, everything changes.

So stop worrying about whether or not you have enough faith! Just decide once and for all that you do. And then act that way. Live your life as someone who believes! How do you do that?

I'm glad you asked. Read on!

13.

Getting Straight with God

So now we come to the hard part.

Maybe you think we've already talked about some difficult things—I disagree. Up till now we really haven't had to make any *sacrifices*. Even deciding to have faith doesn't cost us anything—at least not in the beginning. But now it's time to start putting some of these random ideas we've been discussing together. And whenever you put something together—especially something magnificent, like your life—you always have to leave something out. It's the leaving-out part that hurts.

In this case, we have to start ruthlessly eliminating some of our pride. Pride is the main reason people aren't sorry for the sins they commit—and that's what we're going to focus on now: being sorry for sins.

Notice I said *sins*. Not faults, not weaknesses, not shortcomings, not any of those words the world uses to make us feel better about ourselves. The world is always trying to confuse us when it comes to this subject. It's always trying to make us ignore the reality of who we are, how we act, and what we do wrong. Well, it's time to get unconfused.

Sinning is the act of offending God. It's doing things that are wrong in *God's* eyes, not necessarily *our* eyes. And that's why people's screens go up so fast whenever we broach this subject. Nobody ever wants to be told that they're doing something wrong. We spoke a little in chapter 3 about our secret self—all the toxic thoughts and desires we keep buried inside and never tell anyone about, because we *know* how horrible they are. But what happens the moment someone else tries to point that fact out? How defensive do we get? How defensive do *you* get?

That's when all the comparisons start flying, isn't it? There's such a thing as "comparison morality." It's when we say things like "Yes, it's true that I've cheated on my spouse, but *compared with* all the other nice things I do, I'm really not so terrible. After all, I'm kind and generous and I always try to help people, so the balance doesn't come out too badly."

The balance! As if life were some kind of financial ledger and our only task was to tabulate our assets and liabilities and make sure the bottom line came out a credit.

We're so muddled in our thinking. Even if what we've

done wrong makes up only a fraction of the overall good we've accomplished, that still doesn't make the wrong things *less wrong*. We've got to stop patting ourselves on the back so much. We all do a lot of good things—and we all do a lot of bad things. The ratio isn't the important thing.

Or sometimes people say, "Hey, I'm not a criminal. Just read the newspaper and look at all those thugs out there—all the thieves and rapists and murderers. I don't do any of that. *Compared to them*, I'm a good person."

See? There we go again! We're so busy looking at other people! We just can't help ourselves. We're always spinning our heads in this direction or that, trying to observe the sins of others. And then we wonder why we get so dizzy and confused. The truth is, there's only one place to look: up, at God. And there's only one question to ask him: "How have I failed you?"

You see, it doesn't matter if we think we're good people. So what if we're good? Congratulations to us! It's wonderful that we've managed to avoid a life of crime. But the morally relevant question to ask is not "How do my sins compare with other people's sins?" It's "What are *my* sins?" That's the only thing that ultimately matters in terms of our peace and happiness.

And this is where the world really works against our happiness. The world is always saying that our problems aren't due to sins at all, but rather to the "guilt" we feel—all that nasty guilt caused by "religion." I'm sure you've heard this before. There's "Christian guilt" and "Catholic guilt" and "Irish guilt" and "Italian guilt" and every other kind of guilt imaginable. According to the world, all of it is unhealthy and psychologically damaging. According to the world, life would be so wonderful if there were no such thing as guilt.

But do you know the truth? That's a lot of baloney! It's impossible to live in a world without guilt. Anytime you have a code of conduct, there's going to be some kind of guilt associated with it—and it doesn't matter what that code is. To be in a family means that you have to follow a certain code of conduct. To be in a friendship means that you have to follow a certain code of conduct. To be at a job means that you have to follow a certain code of conduct. To be in a romantic relationship means that you have to follow a certain code of conduct.

And guess what? If you fail to live up to the code of conduct you're supposed to follow, you're going to experience some form of guilt. Whenever you have rules of *any* kind, there are bound to be people who feel guilty when they *break* those rules. That's just common sense.

Do you think Hollywood has its own "moral" code of conduct, for instance—its own belief system about what's right and wrong, what's sacred and what's okay to attack or lampoon? You bet your life it does! And if you work in the movie business and you violate that code (for example, if you attend a pro-life rally or stand up for prayer in school), you can be sure there are going to be serious repercussions for your career—*unless* you express a certain amount of guilt and contrition.

The point is that when the world voices its "concern" about Christian guilt, it doesn't object one bit to the guilt itself. Let's stop being naïve! What it objects to is the code of conduct—the Christian code of conduct. It objects to the Ten Commandments, the moral teachings of Christ in the gospels, the moral teachings proclaimed by the Christian church for the last two thousand years. *That's* what the world despises.

What the world doesn't realize, of course, is that the Christian code isn't just some collection of manmade rules and regulations designed to make us feel bad. It's the way God meant us to live. It's the code that God himself created, and it's one that's been written into the hearts of every man and woman on the planet. So when we violate it, there are bound to be feelings of guilt, at least on some level.

This whole question really comes back to the reality of sin and what it does to us. We mentioned earlier that sinning causes a kind of spiritual chaos in our souls—a disintegration, a division. It actually "separates" us on three different levels. First, it separates us from ourselves—from who we truly are in God's eyes. Second, it separates us from other people, causing friction and sometimes even havoc in our personal relationships. Finally, it separates us from God himself who is the very opposite of sin.

Every single time we sin, these three divisions take place—and it affects us! Christ himself said that a house divided against itself cannot stand. So what do you think happens when we keep chopping ourselves up in this fashion over a long period of time? We collapse. We crumble. We implode. No one has to tell us to feel unhappy. No one has to tell us to feel guilty. It happens all on its own—because it's built into our very nature.

Now what we do with those guilty feelings is up to us. And this is where we have a few critical decisions to make—because the guilt we feel can either be destructive, or it can be fruitful.

Some people try to ignore their guilt and learn to live with it. After all, you can learn to live with practically anything in life, can't you? But it's hard. It's always there, right under the surface, eating away at you. And many times you might not even know the reason. It's almost like having termites in your house. They can infest the wood structure for years without ever being discovered. You can put all kinds of money into remodeling the exterior of your home and making everything so beautiful on the outside. But meanwhile, beneath the glittering façade the whole thing is coming to pieces.

That's exactly what some people do to themselves. They make lots of money and achieve lots of success in the eyes of the world, and they're still not happy. Then they go to psychologists or take personal development courses, and they sometimes seem to make progress—for a while—but once the emotional high wears off they're no happier than they were before. And the reason is that they haven't addressed the root problem—*not their guilt*, but their sins.

Then there are people who *do* realize they've done something morally wrong and regret it. But the regret they feel is a very *human* kind. They regret that they did something that got them into trouble. They regret that they got caught. They essentially feel stupid and frustrated and angry at themselves.

Whenever people experience this kind of regret they always have a tendency to focus inward and dwell on the actual sins they committed. Have you ever done that? Have you ever played your sins over and over again in your head like a broken record, until you've worked yourself up into a kind of hopeless remorse? There's really no way out of that kind of thinking. It's an infinite loop of frustration and self-recrimination. So many people go through life that way. They're just content to stew in their own guilt, to lie there feeling helpless in a puddle of mud without making any real effort to get out.

Finally, there are people who take a different approach—

a sensible approach. These folks know they've done something wrong and regret it, but instead of focusing inward on their own guilt and sins, they go *outside* themselves—to God. Instead of letting their regret turn into hopeless despair, they lift their heads up to heaven and say, "Lord, I'm sorry. Please forgive me." In other words, they make a *decision*—based on their faith in God and their hope in his mercy—to explicitly confess their sins and ask for forgiveness.

And guess what? God forgives them. Every single time.

Once you get over your own pride, being forgiven for your sins is actually the easiest thing in the world. God *wants* to make it easy for you. He wants to have mercy on you. He wants to help you move quickly from regret to reconciliation. He knows that once reconciliation takes place, healing can finally begin.

Healing, as we all know, is very different from forgiveness. Forgiveness is an "event," something God does for you at a specific moment, when you ask him for it and when you're correctly disposed to it. Healing, on the other hand, is a *process*—sometimes a long and difficult process. But it's a process that's necessary.

Here's an easy way to understand it. If you take a hammer and drive a nail into the wall, you can remove the nail, but there's still going to be a hole there, right? Likewise, if you've been forgiven for a sin, there's still going to be an open wound that remains. Sometimes the wound is leftover emotional pain. Sometimes it's a broken relationship. Sometimes it's the need for some kind of reparation or restitution. Whatever it is, the wound has to be healed, just as the hole from the nail has to be filled. It's the same principle.

The good news is that once God forgives you, he also gives you all the grace you require to go through the healing process—all the humility, all the peace, all the patience, all the perseverance, all the hope, all the wisdom, all the love that you need. It's in receiving all these *other* spiritual graces that you can grow as a human being and experience greater peace and happiness.

You see, unlike human regret, true reconciliation always leads to happiness because it always leads to greater union with God, and as we've said before in this book, union with God is the key to everything in life. Therefore, if you've made the decision to have faith, the next decision should be simple. You should decide to give him your sins, too— every single one. You should confess them and ask for forgiveness—and keep on asking whenever you fall, no matter how many times you fall.

I know I sound like some preacher now, but there's really nothing more important that all of us can do than ask for forgiveness. I say "all of us" because we're all sinners. We've all got to stop this nonsense of blaming other people for our guilt. We've all got to stop letting our pride get in the way of our relationship with God. We've all got to relinquish ourselves. We've all got to wipe the slate clean— to completely surrender. It doesn't matter how many times we've committed a particular sin. Once it's been forgiven, it's gone forever—along with all the other sins, offenses, obscenities, evils, and bad behavior of our past life—all of it gone and forgotten; dead and crucified.

That's right—gone forever. That's the teaching of Christianity. The Bible makes the solemn promise that once God forgives us, he "casts all our sins into the depths of the ocean." And to that line, some spiritual writers have added: "Then God places a sign there that says: *No Fishing Allowed!*"

14.

Free as a Bird

Let's take a quick moment to recap the last two chapters.

We've been discussing spiritual decisions: specifically, the decision to have faith, and the decision to repent of our sins. We're going to add a third one now: the decision to forgive people when they sin against us. These three decisions really make up one piece.

Some people don't understand that. They think that *all* you need to get to heaven is faith in God. And in a sense, that's true. But it really depends on what you mean by faith. Faith *isn't* just believing in God. After all, the devil believes in God, doesn't he? And so do all the demons. And so do many, many evil people right here on earth. They believe in him, but they hate him.

"Belief" is just one part of the faith equation. Real faith involves not just accepting God's existence—but actually turning *to* God and *away* from sin. It's an attempt to be in ever-greater union with God. It's an embrace of godliness. And in order to do that, you have to be sorry when you sin, and you have to forgive others when they sin against you. So there are really three separate components to the one faith decision.

If you like, you can think of faith as a bird. The body of the bird is our belief in God's existence. But a bird also has two wings—and those wings are repentance and forgiveness.

Now, can a bird fly without his wings? Or can he fly with just one of his wings? Of course not. In order for a bird to get off the ground and fly up to the sky, he's got to use both wings. And not just once, but all the time. He has to keep flapping his wings, over and over again. When he stops using both wings, he stops flying. The same is true for us. When we stop repenting of our sins and when we stop forgiving others, we stop flying. And not only that, but we crash to the ground.

Let's talk about this second "wing" for a moment— forgiving others. A very experienced Christian counselor once told me that he thought eighty to ninety percent of the problems people face are the result of their unwillingness to forgive others. The reason he believed that—and why I agree with him—is that when you withhold your forgiveness, you cut yourself off from God's grace and make it very difficult for him to help you with all the other challenges you have in life, whether they're emotional, relational, marital, financial, or psychological in nature. Cutting yourself off from God's grace is like cutting the anchor line from your boat when you're in the middle of a stormy sea. It's dangerous. And that's why you really have to think twice before you withhold your forgiveness from anyone.

There's an awful lot of confusion surrounding the topic of forgiveness. Many people have a mistaken notion of what it means to forgive someone and what it doesn't mean. Forgiveness does *not* mean that you give up your right to self-defense. Everyone has the right to protect themselves from harm, from abuse, from lies, from slander. If you're in some kind of abusive relationship now, God doesn't expect you to stay in it. He expects you to change it, or leave it. Never forget that you have an immortal soul and are made in the image and likeness of God. You have more value than all the stars and planets in the universe put together. You should *never* be a doormat for anyone.

Forgiveness also doesn't have anything to do with good feelings. As we've said before, it's impossible for human beings to have full control over their emotions. If someone hurts you badly, God doesn't expect you to feel all warm and fuzzy toward that person. Nor do you have to respect what that person did. When someone does something wicked, it deserves condemnation. Forgiving someone doesn't ever mean calling evil good. That's a lie. And God never lies.

The fact is that forgiveness doesn't reside in the emotions at all, but rather, in the *will*. If you had to calmly decide the destiny of the person who harmed you, what choice would you make? That's the kind of thing God is interested in knowing. It's perfectly okay to want bad people to be brought to justice on earth if they've done something wrong or criminal. But what you can't ever do is wish *evil* upon them. You can't hope that they get a disease or go to hell. That's up to God—not you.

Forgiveness basically means that even if you have negative feelings toward certain people, you still wish them well; in fact, you still wish them the greatest possible good, which is heaven. It means that even if you're revolted by the thought of those people, you still hope that they embrace God, that they're sorry for their sins, and that they ultimately receive salvation. Christ spelled it out very clearly when he said that we have to "love our enemies and pray for those who persecute us." Praying is really the acid test when it comes to forgiveness. It's the bare minimum we have to do for those who have hurt us.

Now, how do you pray for people who have hurt you—maybe even hurt you badly or abused you?

In some cases it can be extraordinarily difficult. In fact sometimes the best and easiest thing to do is simply pray that God deals with those people in his own way; in whatever way that he—not you—deems best. After all, God knows the evil that they've done, and he knows the proper way to handle them.

You can also pray that they realize the error of their ways. If they're engaging in some kind of bad behavior you can ask God to change their hearts. Or you can pray that God gives *you* the grace to stop disliking them so much; that God heals you and helps you to forgive them; that God gives you the strength and confidence to relinquish your own pain and trust in *his* justice.

If you can't even do *that*, then your hatred has gone so far that it really has separated you from God. Remember, God wills good for everyone—even those who are evil. Yes, God ultimately brings them to justice, but he doesn't hate them. He wants them to be saved. As the Bible says, God makes the rain fall on the good and the bad. And we're called to be in union with God—to imitate him. So if certain people cause you to despise them so much that you're no longer able to do what God wants you to do, those people have effectively separated you from him. That's something you can't allow to happen. You can't give anyone—especially your enemies—the power to interfere with your relationship with God.

And there's really no reason to. Once again, forgiveness is not a feeling. When Christ was hanging on the cross he said, "Forgive them, Father, for they know not what they do." He didn't feel good at that moment. How could he? He was gasping for air and bleeding to death. He was in agony. His friends had abandoned him and everyone around him was mocking him, spitting on him, and cursing him. There's just no way Christ could have felt very friendly or forgiving as he was being crucified. But that didn't stop him from making the decision right there and then to pray for the people who were persecuting him. When he was suffering most, he made sure he didn't exclude anyone from his love or his prayers or his forgiveness.

And neither should you. Forgiveness is one of the most essential parts of the Christian faith. You can't even pray the "Our Father" if you're unwilling to forgive others. Think about what that prayer says: "Forgive us our trespasses as we forgive those who trespass against us." When you say those words, you're basically asking God to forgive you in the exact same way that you forgive other people. So if you can't forgive your mother-in-law or your sister or your cousin because they've done something bad to you, then you can't expect God to forgive you, either. He's going to treat you the same way you treat others. In fact, when you pray the "Our Father" in an unforgiving state of mind, you're actually asking God *not* to forgive you!

And guess what? He won't!

Do you think that's cruel? It's not. It's the only way God

can be fair. There's a great parable in the gospels that illustrates this point perfectly. It's about a servant who owes his master a tremendous amount of money—the Bible says "10,000 bags of gold," but in today's currency it would probably be something like $9 million. The master demands payment but the servant begs him on his knees to give him more time. The master, a merciful man, is moved to pity and forgives him the entire debt. Naturally the man is overjoyed, but on his way out of the master's house, he happens to run into a fellow servant, who owes him one hundred silver coins—in today's money, a mere fifteen dollars. The man grabs his fellow servant by the neck and demands to be paid what he's owed. The servant begs him to be patient, but the man is ruthless. He actually throws the servant into prison until he can repay the debt.

Now, when the friends of the servant hear about this, they're outraged. They go to the master and tell him what's happened. The master, seeing how unmerciful his servant has been, unleashes all his fury on him: "You wicked servant," he says. "I cancelled that debt of yours because you begged me to. Shouldn't you have had mercy on your fellow servant just as I had on you?" And in his anger, he hands the man over to the jailers to be tortured.

So what does this story mean? Obviously it's about us. We're the ones who owe our master—God—a tremendous debt, in fact an infinite debt. God gave us our very lives. We can't ever pay him back for that. And instead of being grateful to him, how do we act? We disobey him all the time, don't we? In fact there's no end to our disobedience. And yet, as we saw in the last chapter, whenever we ask God for forgiveness, he grants it. He not only welcomes us back with open arms, but he offers us eternal life in heaven. In other words, God gives us everything *and* forgives us everything.

And meanwhile, when our "fellow servants" sin against us, what do we do? We throw the book at them! We refuse to forgive them. We put a big X on them. *We're* the wicked, unmerciful servants of the parable. We're the ones who have been forgiven a $9 million debt, and then refuse to forgive the measly fifteen dollars that's owed to us! It's really incredible.

Well, how do you think God is going to treat us for acting this way? In the gospel story, the master hands the man over to the torturers. That sounds pretty harsh. But in truth, that's exactly what happens to us when we become hardened by unforgiveness. We cut ourselves off from God and all his graces. Therefore we cut ourselves off from the possibility of healing, and from the peace and happiness that come from healing. Essentially, we hand ourselves over to "torturers" of a different kind—torturers of fear and loneliness and alienation and boredom and stress and anxiety and depression and frustration. When we purposely separate ourselves from God, that's the kind of life we're doomed to live, irrespective of how much money we make or success we achieve.

Once and for all, we're called to forgive everyone who sins against us, every time they sin against us. We're called to forgive *all* sins—even the most painful ones. We're called to forgive people even if they never ask us for forgiveness, even if they're not sorry, and even if they *keep* sinning against us. We're called to be *perfect* in our forgiveness.

Is that hard to do? Of course it is! In fact it's impossible, humanly speaking. But remember the old saying, "To err is human, to forgive, divine"? That's actually a statement of fact. Forgiveness really is divine. It's from God. And we know that nothing is impossible for God—*or* for us when we're acting in union with him.

So before you go on to the next section of this book, my suggestion is this: Why not try being divine for a change? Why not wipe the slate totally clean? Why not unload all the baggage of unforgiven sins that you've accumulated over the years? Why not make a decision here and now to forgive everyone who's ever hurt you?

It's so simple to do. All you have to say is the following: "With God's help, I decide to forgive _____ for _____."

Fill in the blanks and keep filling them in until you've forgiven absolutely every person you have a grievance against. When you finish, I guarantee you'll be surprised by the burden of weight that's been lifted from your shoulders. And when you try to flap those two wings we talked about earlier, you'll be amazed to see how easy it is to achieve takeoff.

PART V

Focus on the Practical

"Perfection is not attainable, but if we chase perfection we can catch excellence. The quality of a person's life is in direct proportion to their commitment to excellence."

—Vince Lombardi

"Nothing is impossible with God."

—Luke 1:37

15.

Gratitude: The Secret to True Wealth

Over the years I've read dozens of self-help books and hundreds of spiritual books, and I can tell you that they all agree on one point. They all insist that it's impossible to be happy in this life if you don't first know how to be grateful for the blessings you already have. As Cicero said, gratitude truly is the "parent of all virtues."

Now I've used the word *happiness* a lot in these pages, but I want to be clear that happiness isn't at all equivalent to "pleasure." It's possible for you to be extremely ungrateful and still experience many of life's pleasures. In fact, if you're an ungrateful type of person, I'd be willing to bet that you *have* experienced many pleasures. It's one of the ironies of life that the least grateful people often lead the most hedonistic lifestyles. They almost become professional pleasure seekers, going from thrill to thrill, searching for that one high that will finally satisfy the deepest yearnings of their soul. Only they never find it, because they don't have the faintest notion of what real happiness is all about. In the end, all the pleasures they experience do them no permanent good and only lead them to greater emptiness and despair.

Though they might not realize it, the main reason they don't have the ability to be happy is that they're not humble enough to appreciate the purest, most basic blessings of life, and so of course they can't appreciate all the other, secondary blessings—like sensory pleasures. The fact never seems to dawn on them that merely multiplying pleasures doesn't solve anything—not when the real problem is that they don't know how to "appreciate" to begin with.

This isn't a difficult principle to understand. It's why we try to teach our children to say "please" and "thank you" whenever we give them things—so that they won't turn out to be ungrateful when they grow up. We want them to understand that they really don't have a "right" to receive nice things. Yes, we want to give them that ice-cream cone—but they don't have a right to it. It's not owed to them. They have to say please and thank you because they need to know that the ice-cream cone—and the video games and computer games and dolls and toys and the rest—are all *gifts*. We give them to our children out of love; out of a desire we have to make them happy. Not just because they want them.

Now, what happens when we don't teach our children to be thankful? They come to *expect* everything, don't they? They come to have no appreciation for the gifts they receive. They come to think that whatever they want, they *deserve*, that whatever they desire is theirs by birthright. And heaven help their hapless parents if they *don't* get what they want! Because that's when the crying starts—and the sulking and the whining and the tantrums. When children aren't taught gratitude they become spoiled—spoiled little brats! Isn't that true? Haven't you ever witnessed the spectacle of a spoiled child throwing a tantrum when he doesn't get what he wants? It's not very pretty, is it?

Well, I hate to break this to you. But guess what most of us are? We're spoiled brats, too—spoiled *adult* brats! Sure, we say please and thank you sometimes—to other adults. But when it comes to being grateful for the most important things in life—for all the true blessings that are given to us on a daily basis—we act exactly the same as ungrateful children.

What I'm going to say now may sound like a cliché, but it's the truest cliché you'll ever hear: Existence is a miracle—*a miracle!* To answer Shakespeare's famous question once and for all, "to be" *is* better than "not to be." By a long shot! And yet people have lost the wonder of existence. They don't really, truly appreciate it—and so all the wonderful things that exist in life have lost their meaning and

power as well. G. K. Chesterton said that until we appreciate the fact that things *might not be*, we won't ever be able to
appreciate the *things that are*. Until we see the background
of darkness, we can't possibly admire the light.

Now let me ask you some questions. How did you *feel*
two thousand years ago when the Roman Empire ruled the
world? How did you *feel* a hundred years ago before you
were even a gleam in your parent's eyes? How did you *feel*
just one moment before you were conceived?

You felt nothing. You thought nothing. You *were*
nothing.

When you go about your usual routine every day and
get caught up in the million tedious details of life, it's
easy to forget this momentous fact. It's easy to slip into a
mode of ingratitude. But you *can't* forget it. You mustn't allow yourself to forget it. You were once nothing and now
you're something. And being something is better than being nothing. Chesterton also said, "When we were children
we were grateful to those who filled our stockings with
presents at Christmas time. Why are we not grateful to
God for filling our stockings with legs?"

True happiness begins and ends with gratitude for *life*.
Everything after that is mere icing on the cake. If you don't
get this point you can forget about happiness. But if you remind yourself of it every day, then at least there's a chance
you can be grateful for the other blessings in your life, too.

We *all* have blessings—even those of us who are suffering. Try a little exercise. Put aside your problems for a second and take a quick inventory of all the good things in your life. I know it might seem corny to do this, but please go ahead anyway.

Do you have your health, for instance? And by that I don't mean, are you free of ailments. I mean, can you breathe on your own, can you walk or move around on your own, can you see and hear what's going on around you? Are you able to eat? Do you have adequate food and shelter?

Do you have the gift of intelligence? Or any other talents? Are you free from serious mental or psychological problems? Are you able to read, to talk, to ask questions, to learn things?

Do you have any family or friends? Anyone you love or who loves you? Have they ever taught you anything? Have they ever done anything kind for you? Have you ever laughed and had fun times with them? What about animals? Have you had any pets? Have you ever been the recipient of the unconditional love of a dog?

What about all the experiences you've had—good and bad? Have they taught you anything? Have any of the really bad experiences ever led to anything positive? What about the country where you've grown up and lived? Do you have rights there? Are you protected by laws? Are there doctors and hospitals in case you get sick? Are there police and fire-fighters in case you're in danger?

How about all the comforts of life? All the wonders of technology? Have you benefited from the advances that have been made the last hundred years—from cell phones and computers and electronic gadgets to all the other modern forms of convenience and travel and entertainment?

What about the beauties of nature? Not just sunsets and mountains and waterfalls and lakes and beaches and oceans, but also the fields of study associated with the natural sciences—like botany and biology and physics and astronomy. Have you ever gotten any enjoyment from just learning about the world?

And finally, what about all the quiet blessings in life? C. S. Lewis often talked about the joy of simply taking a walk in the woods, or reading a good book, or drinking a cup of hot cocoa on a winter's night. Ernest Hemingway wrote about the pleasure of just sitting at an outdoor café, watching the light change in the twilight.

All of these are blessings from God. And all of them should be appreciated for what they are: freely bestowed gifts.

But there's even more. Because gratitude doesn't just pertain to *natural* things. It has a spiritual dimension, too. God has given us *supernatural* blessings that are even greater than food, family, and friends.

As Christians we believe that by virtue of Christ's sacrifice on the cross, we've become the adopted children of God. We're not just intelligent animals, high up on the evolutionary food chain—we're actually sons and daughters of God. That means we share in God's life—God's divine, *immortal* life. It means we can love with the same kind of love God has—a superhuman love. It means we can have superhuman faith and hope. It means that even if our lives are full of turmoil, we can have a peace that the Bible says "transcends all understanding."

It means that when we sin, we can be forgiven—easily; it means that God's mercy is always available to us, no matter what we do. So often Christians take this for granted. They take Christianity itself for granted. They don't realize what a privilege it is to have the true faith, to belong to Jesus Christ, to be able to know God intimately and personally through his son and through his Word and through his church.

Most important, they take it for granted that we've been saved from a death that lasts forever. Christians believe in the Resurrection. That means that someday we're going to rise from the dead. Actually *rise from the dead*. All the things we desire now—money, power, status, fame, luxuries—are all nothing in comparison to the joy that awaits us in heaven. This isn't wishful thinking or fantasy. It's what Christianity is all about. Someday, in heaven, we're really going to see our loved ones again, and we'll be able to live together with them in a place that's free from all pain and sickness and sadness—forever.

Do you think that's something to be grateful for? Yet we hardly ever think about it. Instead, all we do is complain, complain, complain about our terrible problems. And that's why we're like spoiled children.

So what's the solution? How do we flick on the "gratitude" switch? It's not always the easiest thing to do. After all, when you have a spoiled child it can be quite difficult to "unspoil" him. It takes a lot of work and doesn't happen overnight. The same is true for us. To cultivate an "attitude of gratitude" it takes practice and discipline.

First of all, to be in a constant state of appreciation, you have to constantly ask yourself the question: What am I grateful for? You need to constantly "count your blessings." You don't necessarily have to go over a full, itemized list all the time—but every day you should at least ask yourself what you're *most* grateful for.

Second, you should force yourself to say "please" and "thank you" more—to God! Grace before meals is just the minimum. Most people don't even do that nowadays— especially when they're at restaurants—because they don't want anyone to think they're "religious fanatics." But Christians should have more guts than that. Chesterton, who spent his whole life writing about gratitude, went even further and said a short prayer of thanksgiving before going to concerts, before reading books, before admiring sunsets, before sketching, swimming, walking, playing, dancing, and even before he put his pen to paper. Why not do the same?

Third, if you want to feel gratitude, you have to sometimes feel what it's like to do without. You have to occasionally deny yourself what you're legitimately permitted to do. In other words, you have to *fast*. Fasting is a powerful way to help you to appreciate the things in life that you take for granted. And I'm not just talking about fasting from particular foods. I'm talking about fasting from *any* activity that you enjoy.

In the same way, you should sometimes force yourself to *do* things that are somewhat inconvenient. If you have a dishwasher, for example, you should occasionally wash the dishes by hand. If you have a car, you should sometimes take the bus to work. I hear people say all the time that they "need" a bigger car because their family is growing. But that's not true. They don't *need* a bigger car. They *want* a bigger car. Just look at the poor woman down the street with four kids, piling onto the bus with bags and a stroller. Sure, it's great to have a bigger car—but only if you appreciate that it's better than having no car at all.

Finally, and most important, gratitude should not only help you to *feel* good, but also inspire you to *do* good. If you really appreciate the blessings you've been given by God, then you should show it by trying to imitate him more. That means being kinder, more patient, more forgiving, more loving, more sacrificial. It means acting more like a true Christian is supposed to act.

Look, I know that all of this is easier said than done. But it's not only critical, it's necessary. Expressing gratitude is the *very essence* of human happiness. A wise man once said that the worst moment in life for an atheist is when he feels truly grateful for something but then realizes he has no one to thank. Fortunately, you and I don't have that problem. We know whom to thank. We just don't thank him enough.

So from this moment forward, why not make a solemn pledge to be more grateful for everything you've been given in life? No matter what your problems, make a real effort to remember that you're *already* rich. You already have more than most people. You already have wealth and abundance. In fact, when it comes to the blessings of God, you're already a billionaire.

16.

Struggling Against Spiritual Gravity

A few chapters ago we talked about the decision to ask God for forgiveness whenever we sin. But we really didn't focus on any kind of practical strategy to deal with sin, itself. That's a big subject—too big for just one chapter—but there is something we need to discuss now if we're going to make any headway in our attempt to attain earthly happiness, and it has to do with the concept of "gravity."

Once, when I was in third grade, there was a science fair at school and all the kids had to put together their own projects and present them to the rest of the class. I wanted to be a doctor from an early age, and I also loved dinosaurs, so science was actually my best subject. But I had a big problem—I was lazy. So I kept procrastinating and procrastinating, and when the day of the fair finally came, I still hadn't done my project. On the morning of my presentation, I desperately tried to come up with something—anything—but my mind was a blank. Then, as I was walking through the schoolyard, I had an idea. I spotted a small, smooth rock that was lying on the ground next to the fence and put it in my pocket before going up to class.

All the other kids seemed to be thoroughly prepared. In fact, some of the science projects looked like they had been designed by NASA engineers, complete with buttons and levers and lights and sound effects. I remember sitting there as each of the students presented their work, and thinking to myself, "I'm really going to look like an idiot."

When my turn finally came, I went to the front of the classroom, pulled the rock out of my pocket, held it in front of me, and said as seriously as I could, "Class, this is just a small rock, but look what happens when I let it go." I then ceremoniously dropped the rock and let it bounce on the floor. Then I looked up and said even more ceremoniously, "Did you see what just happened? The rock I was holding didn't float up into the air when I dropped it. No. It fell to the floor. I have just demonstrated one of the most important principles in all science: the law of gravity. If it wasn't for the law of gravity, all of you would fly out of your seats right now and shoot into outer space."

That's exactly what I said—or words to that effect. Then I explained what I remembered from my own reading about gravity. I even told them the legendary story about how Sir

Isaac Newton "discovered" gravity one day when he was sitting under an apple tree reading a book, and an apple suddenly fell from one of the branches above him, conking him on the head.

My "presentation" amused some of the kids, but my teacher wasn't fooled at all. She gave me an Incomplete for not doing my assignment properly. And of course she was right. Laziness should never be rewarded. But as the years passed, I've realized something interesting. I've realized that what I said to my classmates that day was actually very significant. In fact, decades after that embarrassing presentation, I find that I'm *still* talking about gravity. Gravity as a principle is so fundamental and so important that it transcends physics and has applications in philosophy, psychology, ethics, and even theology. And the reason is that all things in life—not just rocks—have a tendency to fall.

This is especially true when it comes to our efforts to be good and virtuous. As we've said already, human resolve can be pretty pathetic sometimes. We all know how easily we fall back into our old habits and vices, and how happily we revel in the mud. I'm not talking about the influence of the devil or demons or dark spiritual forces. We'll get to *that* later in this book. Right now I'm just talking about the tendency human beings have to sink to their lowest level. I'm talking about *spiritual gravity*. Most psychologists and personal development experts don't seem to get this concept. They attribute our moral setbacks to false guilt, or neuroses, or insecurities, or a hundred other things. But they never hit the nail on the head. Only the great world religions— especially Christianity—have identified the problem for what it truly is: a universal tendency to sin, caused by something in our own human nature that's broken, tainted, and fallen.

Remember the story of Adam and Eve in the Garden of Eden? Our secular culture dismisses it as a silly myth. But it's not. There are many profound spiritual truths contained in that story. Recall that in the book of Genesis, God created the first man and woman and placed them in the middle of Paradise. At the time there was no such thing as suffering or death. Adam and Eve were happy, and God gave them complete freedom to do anything they liked— except one thing. He forbade them to eat from a certain tree in the middle of the garden, because he said its fruit would kill them. That's really the key point to understand. What God was essentially saying was that human beings were created to have a lot of freedom. But there are *limits* to that freedom. You can't do anything you want, anytime you want. That's not freedom at all—it's license.

Well, we know how the story ended. Adam and Eve chose to disobey God and eat the forbidden fruit. And it was because of that free, prideful decision that evil and suffering entered the world and were passed on to future generations of mankind. In rejecting God, our first parents lost everything that went along with being in union with God—including perfect happiness on earth—and what they gained was sickness, corruption, war, loneliness, old age, and death.

And they got something else, too: a weakened human will and a tendency to sin that we just talked about. Theologians call it *concupiscence*, and unless you understand that every human is subject to it, you'll never grasp why simple self-improvement techniques and other forms of psychological therapy never seem to work permanently. No matter how motivated you may be to change for the better, and no matter how much progress you make, there's always a force trying to drag us down. There's always a "crack" in our moral armor. There's always a natural *disposition* we have to sin. It's part of our very nature and originated when human beings first fell from God's grace.

That's why humility is so important in spiritual life. Having humility means that you understand how *vulnerable* you are to making mistakes. After all, you're a weak, sinful, fallen human being. You're not perfect, and you never will be. When you're truly humble, you're not surprised when you commit a sin—even if it's an extremely serious sin, and even if you've committed the same sin many times.

That doesn't mean you're not sorry, or that you're not

committed to changing. Of course you have to change. Of course you have to make progress and become more disciplined and more virtuous. Of course you have to firmly resolve to turn away from your sins. That's one of the prerequisites of being forgiven—the decision to try to stop your bad behavior. But at the *very same time* you have to recognize the truth that you're really just a puny, powerless human being and don't have any real strength apart from what God gives you when you're in union with him.

Believe me, if you fall into despair over some offense you've committed, it's a sure sign of spiritual pride. It's a sure sign that you think you're stronger than you actually are. If you were truly humble, you would never beat yourself up. Instead, you would *pick yourself up* and try your best not to do it again.

I can't say this strongly enough. When it comes to your moral failures, you've got to employ what Mother Angelica, the feisty little nun who founded the Eternal Word Television Network, called the "D and D" system—"do it and drop it." You've got to try with all your might to resist temptation, but if you give in and "do" it, then you've got to immediately say you're sorry and "drop" it. You should never get too upset, and never, ever lose hope in God's mercy. Remember, God's been watching human beings commit the same sins for thousands of years. There's nothing you can do that will shock him. He's seen it *all*.

Now, of course, the best thing to do when faced with any kind of immoral temptation is to stomp it out before it gets too strong. And this is another point I want to talk about. It might seem obvious, but all "big" sins in life start out very "small." A tiny decision to engage in some "harmless" flirtation at the office can put a process in motion that eventually leads to an extramarital affair. A little "fudging" on the books to avoid an embarrassing financial situation can eventually lead to tax fraud. A choice to keep brooding over a frustrating family problem can lead to a terrible outburst of anger and a rupture in family relations. A decision to have one beer when you know you have an alcohol problem can result in a month-long binge and the loss of your job.

Every decision to do something wrong, no matter how small, has a moral trajectory of its own and the potential to lead to a much bigger problem later on. And if you fall in a serious way—for instance, commit adultery, steal from someone, violently lose your temper, etc.—it's always the result of many smaller falls that took place beforehand.

So if you want to avoid the big falls, you've got to work on those smaller ones first! Doesn't that make sense? If there's an intruder at the door, and he wants to come in and hurt you, you've got to keep the door locked and bolted. The moment you open it—even an inch—

you've given the intruder a chance to force his way in. And the more you open it, the harder it is to keep it closed; the harder it is to resist the power of the intruder as he pushes his way through. The only way to really prevent a break-in is to stop it at the beginning. Or as Tony Robbins used to say, you have to "kill the monster when it's little."

If you don't, it can lead to all kinds of problems. Not only bigger sins, but habitual sins as well, and compulsions, and even serious addictions. Anyone suffering from an addiction—whether it's drugs or alcohol or gambling or sex—knows how much havoc it can wreak in a person's life. Addictions can destroy your health, your self-esteem, your family and friendships; they can sap all your energy, rob you of your emotional and spiritual power, and cause you to waste years and even decades of your life. They're deadly in every way.

Have you ever seen a gerbil when it's in a cage, running on one of those spinning wheels? Sometimes people who have addictions feel just like that. Once they start to binge—once they get caught on that wheel of compulsion—it's almost impossible for them to stop. Either they have to be thrown off because of some huge problem that their behavior has caused, or they literally fall off from exhaustion. Then they go through this same cycle again—binging, getting into trouble, breaking down from guilt or exhaustion, recuperating for a time, and then starting over.

It's a terrible way to live. Sometimes these poor people really sink into despair. They think God hates them and could never forgive them for their sins. But, of course, God loves them and is *always* anxious to forgive them. He understands them and their compulsions better than they understand themselves—he knows they aren't giving the full, free consent of their will when they fall into temptation. He knows they're being *compelled* by their own habit, and so he forgives them when they're sorry—even if they fall a million times.

But that doesn't change the fact that addictions cause damage. Yes, God's mercy is infinite, and he'll always help in the healing process that follows a person's falls, but he isn't going to completely erase the destruction that's been done. And he won't always restore the precious time that's been lost in the person's life.

For these reasons and more, if you've got some kind of unhealthy compulsion or addiction, you've got to make it your first priority in life to seek professional help—*now*! You can't wait another week or even another day. It's beyond the scope of this book to solve these kinds of problems. In fact, you can follow all the advice this book has to offer and still be unhappy if you have some kind of serious addiction and fail to deal with it. You've simply got to bite the bullet and find someone who can help you. In this digital world of ours—this "information age"—there's no excuse not to. You're literally one click away from expert assistance for any problem you may have. All you need is Internet access, and that's available free of charge in libraries across the country.

Here's just one example of a practical "tip" you can learn by going on the Internet. Have you ever heard of the acronym "H.A.L.T."? When compulsive cravings strike, psychologists tell us that the four most common "triggers" are hunger (H), anger (A), loneliness (L), and tiredness (T). If you experience any of these states for long periods of time—and you have a tendency to compulsive behavior—then those compulsions are very liable to flare up. In other words, each one of these four conditions, if not dealt with, can make you vulnerable to addictive relapse. On the other hand, if you address these conditions—the hunger, the anger, the loneliness, the tiredness—then the compulsive cravings will often begin to melt away. Not all the time, but often.

Even if you don't have an addiction, you know this is true. Haven't you ever wanted to bite off someone's head just because you hadn't had your lunch and were feeling grumpy? Or because you hadn't gotten enough sleep the night before? Or because you were angry about an unrelated problem with your boss or your spouse?

Of course you have. We all have. But if you suffer from a serious compulsion or addiction, then you have to be even more careful to avoid these vulnerable states. The result might not just be that you snap at someone. The result might be that you go on a binge; that you start running on that terrible wheel of compulsion again, with drugs or alcohol or gambling or sex or whatever it is you habitually use to obtain relief and pleasure.

The bottom line is that you have to keep the word H.A.L.T. in mind at all times. You have to make sure you don't go for long periods without eating when you're hungry; you have to deal with any unresolved problems in your life that might be making you angry; you have to reach out to other people and get involved in different social activities in order to avoid loneliness; you have to do everything in your power to get enough sleep and rest. In other words, you have to make sure you're taking good care of your *physical and emotional well-being.*

Listen, I know all of this is a lot to get your mind around. But it's part of the process of living your life to the fullest. Let me try to summarize what we've said here very briefly.

No matter what you accomplish in life, no matter how successful or wonderful you become, you have to understand that there's always going to be a force trying to pull you down, a spiritual gravity. It's part of our fallen human nature. You have to recognize this tendency to sin, be humble about it, and never lose your self-esteem because of it. Life is going to be a moral struggle for you and everyone else you know to the very end—and you're going to have to be willing to fight, fall, repent of your sins, and get back up again many times.

When you do get back up, you're going to have to resolve that the next time you're faced with temptations—even tiny ones—you're not going to wait till later to deal with them. You're going to squash them now, while you can still overpower them. You're going to slam the door shut on any potential threat. You're going to treat even the smallest sins as if they were deadly spiders—no more thinking, no more hesitating. Stomp on them and kill them—before they kill you!

Finally, if you do find yourself in the unfortunate position of suffering from a compulsion or addiction, you're not going to lose your self worth and self esteem. You're going to H.A.L.T., take a deep breath, look at your life, and try to address any underlying emotional or physical problems that might be fueling the addiction. Most important, you're not going to be too prideful to seek professional help. You're going to resolve to be strong and fight this addiction, not by yourself but with the help of family, friends, experts—and God Almighty.

We're going to talk more about divine assistance in a

little while. After all, there are some powerful spiritual weapons you can employ to help overcome even the worst problems. But right now, let's switch gears for a moment and handle a couple of practical "housekeeping" matters having to do with your health and finances.

17.

Health: A Commonsense Approach

That's right. It's time to focus again on health.

The reason is that in the next few chapters we're going to be talking about some things that are very difficult to do. And it takes a certain amount of vitality and energy to do difficult things—even difficult spiritual things.

I said back in chapter 9 that the Christian attitude toward health is somewhat paradoxical. On the one hand, we know that "the body is the temple of the Holy Spirit" and therefore must be treated with the greatest respect. That includes taking care of it with proper nutrition and exercise, and not abusing it with drugs or excessive alcohol. On the other hand, we're not ever supposed to forget that our real home is heaven, and that our life on earth could end at any time. Therefore we should never cling to our bodies as if they were the most important things in the world. We always have to have our "bags packed," so to speak—because we could be called home at any moment.

If you're able to understand and embrace both these truths at the same time, then you're in a good position to lead an *authentically* healthy life—one that neither overemphasizes bodily health nor neglects it.

With that in mind, I'd like to try to simplify the subject of health for you. Bear in mind that I'm not a doctor, and what follows is neither a weight loss plan nor a fitness program. It's just my personal attempt to inject some common sense into the whole, confused discussion of health. After all, there seem to be thousands of health books out there and many of them are making statements that totally contradict each other. You know the kind of thing I mean: One study shows that soy protein is bad for you; another shows that it's good for you. One expert advocates low-carb diets, another high-carb diets. One book "conclusively" proves that large doses of vitamin C are incredibly beneficial; another proves they're a waste—again "conclusively."

How do we make sense of it all?

The first thing to do, I think, is to take a step back and look at the entire health picture. When you do that, you realize that there are really only four major pieces to the puzzle—only four factors that ultimately determine a person's health and longevity. They are, in order of importance: 1) genetics, 2) psychology/stress, 3) exercise, and 4) nutrition.

Let's take them one at a time. First: genetics.

There's not much anyone can do about his or her genetics, is there? When you were conceived in your mother's womb, you were dealt a certain genetic "hand." For some people the hand was good, for some mixed, for some poor. Whatever cards you've been dealt, you're pretty much stuck with them. But being stuck with your genetics doesn't mean you can't do anything to affect your health. You can. Remember the story *A Christmas Carol*, by Charles Dickens? Remember what Scrooge says to the Ghost of "Christmas Yet to Come," after the ghost shows him a vision of all the terrible things that are going to happen to him? Scrooge asks the ghost, "Are these the shadows of things that will be, or the shadow of things that *might* be?"

The answer, of course, is that Scrooge *does* have a chance to alter the future; that even though he's on a path to death and damnation, he *is* able to change his destiny—by changing his ways. The same is true for us in regard to genetics. Yes, you may have "predispositions" to certain diseases. But a predisposition is not the same as the disease itself. It's only a "shadow of something that *might* be." Therefore you can do something about it. If you know your family's medical history, you can take whatever preventative measures are available. For example, if you have diabetes in your family, you can watch your sugar intake and focus on doing lots of exercise. If you have heart disease in your family, you can try to eliminate most fatty foods from your diet. If there's cancer in your family, you can make sure you go in for early testing. In other words, by simply being aware of your genetic predispositions, you can take some common-sense actions that might prolong your life for decades.

Another important thing for you to understand is that God *knows* your genetic code. He knew it from the beginning of time and allowed it to be programmed exactly as it is. Therefore it's the *perfect* genetic code for you. No matter what physical challenges might result from your heredity, you can be sure that they can all help you fulfill God's will and lead you to peace, happiness, and eventually heaven. So there's no reason for you to ever be overly frightened. Instead, you can just bring the matter to prayer, like everything else that's important in your life. You can ask God to protect you from any genetic predispositions you may have—especially if preserving your health might help you to serve God more perfectly.

And it might! I know people whose whole families have been decimated by cancer and yet have lived well into their nineties. There's such a thing as the "God gene," and it outweighs and outranks every other kind of gene in your genetic code. If it's God's will that you beat the family odds and live to 104, you will—period.

The second major factor affecting your health is your psychology—especially your stress levels. After genetics, this is really the most important thing in determining how you feel and how long you live. It's much more critical than vitamins and minerals and all those products people spend so much money on, trying to stay young.

Why? Because stress causes acid. Stress causes cell mutation. Stress causes toxins. Stress causes wrinkles and gray hairs. Stress causes breakdown at every level. This is a scientific fact. There's no dispute over it. It's much more important to avoid stress than it is to avoid hamburgers! Stress will cause you to have a heart attack a lot faster.

That's why it's funny sometimes when you see health fanatics get so frustrated if they're not able to order their tofu or their "omega-three eggs" when they're out at a restaurant. They don't realize how silly they're being. The stress they're experiencing over their diet probably causes more of their cells to mutate than if they had just eaten a simple, relaxed meal—even an unhealthy one. For all their zeal, they don't understand the simple fact that "irritation equals mutation," that anxiety is a much bigger killer than food.

So what should you do to avoid stress? The answer is—anything and everything! Unlike your genetic makeup, this *is* something you can change. There are lots of free resources on stress reduction that are available to anyone with Internet access or the ability to walk to a library. All you have to do is make use of them. Whether it's deep-breathing exercises or relaxing music or laughter therapy or physical activity or meditation, there's something out there that can help you—no matter how serious your personal problems.

And don't be surprised if the simplest solutions work best. Thomas Aquinas, one of the greatest theologians and philosophers who ever lived, said that "a good sleep, a bath, and a single glass of wine" is sometimes the best way to decrease sorrow and anxiety. Indeed, the power of sleep should *never* be underestimated. If you feel like an emotional wreck sometimes, it may just be that you're not getting enough rest. When you sleep well you're able to handle all of life's problems better. Sleep is refreshing. Sleep is holy. The Bible talks about Christ sleeping on several occasions—once when he and the apostles were on a small boat and a storm was raging on the sea. The apostles were all so worried that the tiny boat was going to sink, but Christ just kept on sleeping right through it. Talk about low-stress!

That's the way *all* of us should be. No matter how great the storm, we have to have confidence that God knows what's best. He may not stop the thunder and lightning, but he'll always see us through it. Christ said that we shouldn't be anxious about *anything*. And if he said it, that means it's possible.

The third major health category is exercise. We've spoken about this already and there's not much more to add here. If you want to live, you have to move. If you want to have energy, you have to expend energy. It's that simple. There's no need to go on any kind of radical, high-intensity fitness program. If you enjoy that kind of thing and can do it without getting injured, fine. But it's not strictly necessary. The only thing that's essential to prevent illnesses and improve your chances of living longer is consistent, low-to-medium-intensity aerobic exercise.

Why is that the key? Because it boosts your immune system. It trains the body to burn calories faster. It makes your heart and lungs stronger. It makes all your systems function more efficiently. There's just no excuse not to do it. If you haven't found a way to work it into your weekly schedule, then you had better figure it out soon. It's not that difficult! If you walk or jog or cycle or swim or play tennis or do anything that gets your heart rate up for thirty to sixty minutes, three or four times a week, and you do it consistently over a period of years, you're going to be getting the maximum health benefits that exercise can offer. Sure, you can do more if you like. Your body can get used to anything, so it's not a bad idea to spice things up and vary your intensity levels every once in a while. But the goal is not to beat yourself up every day. It's to be consistent. It's to be injury-free. It's to be able to exercise till the end of your days.

The last health category is nutrition, and it's probably

the area that needs simplifying the most. The reason is that there are a dizzying number of diets and food-based health programs on the market. Many of them have whole industries built up around them. Navigating through the maze isn't easy. There are "detox" diets, "beauty" diets, "alkaline" diets, "anti-inflammatory" diets, "food-combining" diets, "vegan" diets, "low-fat" diets, "low-calorie" diets, "low-carb" diets, "nondairy" diets, "nongluten" diets, etc. The list is just endless.

But can I tell you something interesting? All these diets have one thing in common. No matter what the nutritional philosophy behind them, they all agree on the importance of eating one very specific kind of food. Can you guess what that food is?

Vegetables. Good old vegetables. That's the one universal and unifying constant amid all the crazy confusion. Vegetables truly are the "super food" of the world. When it comes to nutrition, they literally do everything. They provide water and oxygen to your cells; they make the body more alkaline and less acidic; they decrease chronic inflammation; they're chock-full of antioxidants, vitamins, and minerals; and they're generally high in fiber, low in calories, and easy to digest.

Do you know that if you did nothing but eat a large vegetable salad along with your lunch and your dinner every single day for the rest of your life, you'd be further along than ninety percent of the general population when it comes to nutritional health? It's true! And you probably wouldn't have to read another health book for the rest of your life.

That simplifies the subject of nutrition quite a bit, doesn't it?

And I'll make things simpler still. Along with eating lots of vegetables, there's one other sensible rule to follow. In fact, it's probably the most important dietary discipline you can ever master. It's called *moderation*, and it simply means limiting the kinds and the quantities of food you eat.

Listen, we all know the foods that are bad for us. We've all heard them repeated ad nauseam. We know that consuming too much sugar and salt and caffeine and red meat and processed foods and fast foods can be very harmful to us. And yet we can't seem to stop. So shouldn't the solution be obvious? Shouldn't the solution be that if we can't stop eating them, we should at least *cut down* on them? Isn't that logical?

Well, that's what moderation is all about: cutting down. The truth is, as long as you don't overeat a particular food, there's no reason to stress over it. Sure, a Big Mac is bad for you. And if you stop for lunch every day at a different fast-food restaurant, your arteries are going to be clogged in a very short time. But if you do it every once in a while, it's just not going to kill you, despite what the health police say.

Or take a more personal example. I'm Italian and I *love*

Italian food. If you put me on one of those low-carb diets and said I could never have pasta again, I'd probably fall to my knees and cry out in agony. After all, what's the point of living in a world without rigatoni? But instead, if you asked me to *cut down* on my pasta—maybe even significantly—and perhaps supplement it occasionally with some of that "omega-three-enriched, whole-wheat pasta," then at least there's a chance I'd listen.

See what I'm trying to get at? The goal is to limit—not eliminate. What we're aiming for here is long-term consistency. And when it comes to your diet, the key to that is moderation.

Is moderation difficult to learn? Sure it is. But it's a heck of a lot easier than trying dozens of different fad diets and never sticking to one. And if you *are* successful in mastering it, you can have any food you want, any time you want—and never have to worry about adverse health effects. That's not a bad deal!

So, to summarize, here's what I believe to be a sensible and practical approach to health:

1. **Genetics**: Know your family history and be aware of any predispositions you have to diseases so you can take preventative action.
2. **Psychology/Stress**: Do research to find a stress reduction method that works for you.

3. **Exercise**: Do low-to-medium-intensity aerobic work for thirty to sixty minutes, three or four days a week.

4. **Nutrition**: Learn moderation in everything—except veggies! Eat truckloads of those.

I want to repeat that I'm not a doctor. I don't have any medical degrees. But I do have something called common sense, and I've spent an enormous amount of time studying this subject. I'm confident that if you follow these tried-and-true guidelines over the course of several years, you'll be safeguarding your health in an extremely proactive and effective way; and yet you won't be making the spiritual mistake of turning health into some kind of religious idol. You'll be keeping it in proper perspective.

And proper perspective is what this book is all about.

18.

Money Matters

In the last chapter I warned you that I wasn't a doctor, and then proceeded to dispense health advice. Now I'm warning you that I'm not a financial planner, and I'm about to give you advice about money!

Believe me, I'd rather not. I'd rather keep things on a more spiritual plane. But I don't think I have a choice. Too many people experience anxiety over this subject. Too many people feel their lives are being ruined because they don't have enough money. So what I want to do is attempt to put this subject in perspective—spiritual perspective—and then lay out in very general terms what I believe to be a commonsense approach to dealing with finances and financial problems.

Regarding perspective, once again there are two extremes to be avoided. One is the belief that having a lot of money is always a good thing. The other is the belief that having a lot of money is always a bad thing. Neither of these is true. Neither is taught by Christianity.

First, let's look at the myth that wealth is always wonderful. You hear this all the time from personal development experts. Oh, how they love to talk about money and the glories of wealth! How incredible it would be if people just lost their "guilt" about having money and concentrated on acquiring as much of it as possible so they could finally live freer, more powerful lives. Some Christian leaders say the same thing. Night and day they preach about the "Gospel of Prosperity," bouncing excitedly about the stage in designer suits, with their Rolex watches and gold cufflinks glittering in the lights. "Everyone can be a billionaire!" they shout. "Everyone *should* be a billionaire. After all, God's riches are abundant, aren't they? And he wants everyone to share in them! All you have to do is have a little faith and come and get it! Do I hear an amen?"

Then you have the opposite camp—those who preach the "Gospel of Poverty." These somber, sullen, unsmiling folks, puritanical to the core, truly believe that money is "the root of all evil" and that everyone who has it is basically on the road to fiery perdition. They point to certain lines in Scripture that warn against riches, take them out of context, and without reference to other teachings, twist their meaning. They end up glorifying not only the poor, but the *state* of being poor. They view wealth itself as a vice—so much so that they get uncomfortable anytime anyone gives them an expensive gift or takes them to a fancy restaurant. After all, how could they possibly enjoy such things when people are starving in Ethiopia?

Of course the truth about money is more nuanced than either extreme. When you read through the Bible, for instance, you see lots of rich people—kings and noblemen and statesman—all following God's will. You see that in the history of Christianity, too—and in the history of the world, itself: rich people who somehow have managed to remain humble and use their God-given wealth to accomplish great good.

On the other hand, we all know there have been evil rich people, too. And when they've been bad, they've been *very* bad. This is where the Bible really makes for terrifying reading—especially if you happen to be wealthy. Because one thing that stands out clearly in Scripture is the *danger* of having riches. Christ talked about it all the time: "Many who are first will be last," he said. "No one can serve two masters...God and money." "What does it profit a man if he gains the whole world, but then suffers the loss of his soul?" And most famously: "It is easier for a camel to go through an eye of a needle than a rich man to enter the Kingdom of Heaven."

The real and ever-present danger that comes with having

money is something the personal development folks always miss. In their eagerness to teach people to "excel" and "achieve," they forget to put up the necessary red flags regarding wealth. And those red flags *are* necessary. G. K. Chesterton once quipped, "To be clever enough to make a billion dollars, you must first be stupid enough to *want* a billion dollars!"

The reason he said that was that he knew the spiritual risks inherent in great wealth. He knew that money has the power to separate us from God in a way that few other things in life can. Money can give us a feeling of false invincibility. It can make us think we have everything we need to be happy and that we don't have to rely on anyone or anything—including God. It gives us a false sense of superiority, too—false because while we may be savvier than other people when it comes to worldly matters, we're not more *valuable* in God's eyes. That homeless drug addict on the street may very well make it into heaven before we do. And he may have a higher, more glorious place in paradise than us.

So, for all these reasons and more, you won't be hearing me preach any sermons on the "Gospel of Prosperity." I simply don't know whether making a fortune would be a good or bad thing for your immortal soul. That's really a spiritual matter between you and God. Only he knows what's best for you in light of eternity.

But there is one thing I know for sure: God doesn't want you to have *anxiety* over money. He doesn't want you to have all the joy and enthusiasm sucked out of your life because of overdue bills. He doesn't want you to be spending the precious little time you have on this planet stressing over little green pieces of paper. I know that for a fact because God doesn't want you to stress over *anything*. He wants all of us to be free from fear and worry.

Did you know that in practically every book of the Bible, God tells us not to be afraid? In fact, the words "fear not" and "don't be afraid" appear more than two hundred times in Scripture. And they're not just suggestions—they're commands. God doesn't just say, Try not to be afraid; he says, *Don't be!*

What you have to understand is that God never gives us a command unless he also gives us the ability to follow that command. And that's what I want to focus on for the remainder of this chapter. Not on wealth or poverty—but on eliminating financial anxiety. Everyone needs to know how to do that. Everyone needs to know they *can* do that. Yes, it's difficult, but it's also just a matter of following some basic financial principles—principles that anyone can master. Remember, one of the main objectives of this book is to remind you of the basics in life and help you to practice them not just once in a while, but *all the time*.

The truth is, I don't know if you're destined to ever

become rich, but I do know that you have the ability to solve all your financial problems and eliminate all your fears about money. God himself has given you that ability, and God himself wants to help you. All you have to do is muster the courage to *take action*—starting now.

How do you do that? Here are four commonsense steps you can follow if money has become a source of anxiety for you:

Step One: Make a decision. You need to stop and say: *"I've had enough! It's not going to be this way anymore! I'm going to change things!"* And even more important, you have to decide that you're not going to blame anyone for your problems. From now on, you're going to take full responsibility for your finances. So many people just blame, blame, blame. They love playing the victim. It's the boss's fault, it's the wife's fault, it's the husband's fault, it's the kids' fault, it's the world's fault.

Sorry, but it's *your* fault!

I know you're probably a good person and don't spend much money on yourself. And maybe you work hard and the economy is bad and there are other factors beyond your control that have influenced your circumstances. But even if all that is true, you're never going to solve your problems if you don't have the attitude that your finances are under your control and nobody else's. You're going to be trapped forever unless you drop all that "woe-is-me" nonsense. You're in charge of managing your money. You're in charge of getting out of the hole if you're in one. It's up to you. No more playing the victim. *No more excuses!*

Step Two: You have to get the problem out into the open. Out of the piles of unopened bills, out of the dark recesses of your mind, out into the light—no matter how painful that might be. So many people have no idea what their real financial situation is. Not a clue. If you asked them, they couldn't tell you what their monthly expenses are, or even what their real income is after taxes. And I'm not just talking about lower- and middle-income people. I'm talking about the wealthy. I'm talking about millionaires who don't really understand their own finances. Oh, they may make a lot of money, but they have no idea where it all goes, or why they can't seem to save more, or why they always seem to be on the brink of disaster. They have accountants and lawyers and bookkeepers and all kinds of high-priced consultants, but they don't *personally* understand where they stand when it comes to their own money.

The only solution is to write everything down, yourself. All of it! All your income; all your expenses—not just bills, but food and gas and nail appointments and everything else you think you need to survive. You've got to start as simply as possible—even if you're very wealthy and own three or four different companies. You've got to have your expenses in one place, with the name of each written clearly, the type, the total amount due, the minimum payments, the due dates—everything—broken down into categories you can understand. And all of this has to be kept in a bound notebook or in a computer folder with clean, organized files. No more stray notes and paper clips and staples! No more nonsense! From now on, you need one designated place for your finances.

I know this sounds like Budgeting 101, but so what? Even millionaires need to do this. And when they don't, they get into problems bigger than yours and end up going bankrupt—or worse. You read about it all the time in the newspapers. So no matter what your situation, you've got to be able to take an accurate snapshot of your financial picture. Everything starts from this picture. You can't successfully move forward without it. Once you have your finances on paper or some kind of electronic file that you can look at in one glance, then you've finally put yourself in a position of control. Finally you're moving events and events aren't moving you. That's a huge advantage. And it leads to the next step.

Step Three: You need to take what you've written and really spend some time reflecting on it. You need to carefully review your expenses and try to understand not only where your money is going but *why* it's going there. This step is all about self-revelation.

And don't be surprised if you discover a lot more about

yourself than you bargained for. Understanding your finances can be a gateway to understanding all kinds of deeper psychological truths about yourself. After all, why are you in debt? What's the real reason? Is it just that you don't make enough money? Or is there another cause? Is it perhaps that you can't say no—to yourself, or your spouse, or your kids? Do you have an underlying problem with depression, and the only thing that gives you any joy is to shop or eat out or gamble? Do you have some kind of addiction that eats away either at your money, or your time, or saps you of the energy and confidence you need to go out and conquer the world?

Or maybe it's not a deeper problem, after all. Maybe you're truly spending the bare minimum and there's just not enough money coming in. But even if that's the case, it's still important to confirm it. Because now you're going to find out what you're capable of as a human being. You're going to make a decision about what you need to do to solve this problem. And that may require something difficult or even heroic on your part. Maybe you need to switch jobs. Maybe you need to get a second job. Maybe you need to get a job beneath your abilities or even your dignity. I don't know what you're supposed to do, but one thing's for sure: you're going to find out what you're made of.

And that's all part of **Step Four**: Come up with a plan of action. How do you clean up the mess? How do you dig yourself out of the hole? How do you move forward as fast as possible to financial freedom?

Obviously I can't lay out that plan for you here. I wish I could. But I don't know your particular circumstances and this isn't a book on finance. I can, however, tell you this: When it comes to the basics, like lowering your debt, there are plenty of terrific, free resources out there. If you go online or visit a library with Internet access, you can quickly find all kinds of budgeting and money management websites. They teach you things like the "snowball" technique, where you pay off your lowest credit card bill first and then use the monthly savings to help pay off the next-lowest bill, and the next lowest, and so on, until the momentum builds like a snowball. That may sound simplistic, but it works. And there are other effective methods just like it.

Once you manage to reduce your debt or at least get to the point where you're not living from paycheck to paycheck, then you can really work at achieving financial freedom. And here's where things get even less confusing, because all the finance books and websites basically teach the same thing. They all say you have to come up with a written budget and *stick to it*—no matter how difficult. They all say you have to create five or six different "buckets" into which you divide your income. They all say you need a "Living Expenses" bucket and an "Emergency" bucket and a "Retirement" bucket and a "Savings" bucket.

They all say you need an "Investment" bucket, too. Remember, *everyone* should be an investor. It doesn't matter who you are; you'll never be well-off or even very comfortable in life if you rely on your salary alone. You have to be able to generate some kind of income in addition to what you earn at work. You have to find some way of making money while you sleep—and the only way to do that is to invest wisely in stocks, bonds, businesses, real estate, etc.

Finally—and perhaps most important—you need to have a "Charity" bucket. God calls everyone to be generous, not just the rich. The gospels are very clear that we're supposed to give out of our need, and not just our abundance. I wrote a book a few years ago called *Ten Prayers God Always Says Yes To*, in which I included a whole chapter on this subject. The simple point I made was that God will *never* be outdone in generosity. When he sees you being generous to others, he will always help you with your problems. Being poor is never an excuse to be stingy when it comes to charity. At a minimum, you should probably donate 10 percent of your net income to those who need it more than you. And believe me, there are *always* people who need it more than you.

So to summarize, here are four simple steps anyone can take to begin solving their financial problems:

1. Make a decision to stop being a "victim";
2. Write down everything so you know where you stand;
3. Reflect on what you've written so you can discover the underlying causes of your financial problems;
4. Come up with a plan of action.

And to these I would add one more step.

5. Focus!

Focus on this area until you get it right! Focus on this area no matter how painful it is! Of course it's going to be painful. Who *wants* to focus on paying bills? It hurts to see how much debt you're in; it hurts to realize unpleasant truths about yourself; it hurts to discipline your spending. It's so much easier to avoid thinking about the subject altogether and live in the state of denial and distraction. So many people do that.

And yet, focusing on this problem is the only way to overcome it. I said earlier in this book that if you wrote just 250 words a day, you could have a novel done in one year. Well, if you seriously reviewed your finances fifteen minutes a day, don't you think that by the end of the year you'd be in better financial shape than you are now? Of course you would! And imagine if you did even more. Imagine if you included God in the equation. Imagine if you asked God every single morning to help you with your finances— not to make you win the lottery or give you a million dollars, but to give you the strength, the perseverance, and the wisdom necessary to fix your problems so that you'll never again feel the anxiety you have now.

Don't you think the One who created the universe and put the stars and planets in motion is smart enough to help you figure out the solution you need? Don't you think that with *his* assistance, you could turn things around?

You don't have to be a financial genius to know that the answer is yes.

19.

Goals and God's Will

It's been said that there are three types of people in the world: those who make things happen, those who watch things happen, and those who *wonder* what happened.

What category do you fall into?

You don't want it to be number two or three, do you? And yet, that's where the bulk of humanity usually ends up spending most of its time.

How do you avoid it? The personal development industry says the answer is to set goals for yourself so you can accomplish great things and "make your dreams into reality." And that's good thinking—as far as it goes. There's a tremendous amount of common sense behind the philosophy of goal setting. So many people have no clue what they want in life, much less how to go about getting it. They really are like ships drifting aimlessly on a vast ocean, floating wherever the prevailing wind happens to take them. Then there are folks who *do* have a general idea what they want, but never get around to the hard work of making their vague desires into specific, achievable objectives. They forget a very simple rule in life: You can't hit a target if you don't have a bull's-eye!

Goal setting gives you that bull's-eye to aim for. Unfortunately, there's a problem with it. A problem the personal development industry—predictably—never brings up. And if you've been reading these chapters closely, you can probably guess what I'm about to say next.

As you carefully map out your own goals, you also have to consider what *God's* goals for you might be. God is already in the future. He already knows what will fulfill you—and what won't. Without taking his will into account, you're only really working on half the equation. That's why so many people who achieve "success" are still unhappy. That's why so many people who are rich and famous still commit suicide. Why would they kill themselves if they had realized all their glittering goals? Obviously their goals didn't make them happy. They got caught in the world's trap. They followed their plan instead of God's.

The question is: What's the best strategy to go about setting your goals, in a way that's both humanly effective and spiritually intelligent? How do you combine the two? There are plenty of books and Internet resources available, as well as workshops and seminars you can take. But what I'd like to do now is give you the basic principles of goal setting. To my mind, there are really only three.

The first and most important rule is that you have to come up with goals that *inspire* you. I know that may sound obvious, but it's amazing how few people do it. Your goals have to be big enough, interesting enough, and exciting enough to make you really want to achieve them. After all, life is tough. There are so many obstacles to overcome. There's just no way you're ever going to accomplish anything significant if you're not willing to endure some real suffering. And the only way to do that is to be motivated enough to push through the pain and tedium and adversity that you're bound to face.

In order to come up with goals that inspire you, you've got to ask yourself some serious questions—and you have to be honest about the answers. What is it that you really want to achieve in life? What is it that you really love? What is it that gives you the most joy? What is it that gives you the most peace? Forget about what the world says you should want. Forget about what's "best" or "most impressive." You have to be brutally honest. What is it that you truly desire in your heart of hearts?

If you're able to come up with a few concrete answers, at least you'll have some indication of what God *might* want for you. God often plants intense desires in our hearts to help lead us where he wants us to go. You can't always be sure they're from him, of course, but if you sincerely get joy and fulfillment from doing something, and it's not sinful, or detrimental to your state in life (as a married person or a parent or a member of the clergy), then it might very well be a sign that God wants you to explore the area more.

So with that in mind, what is it you really want? And even more important, why do you want it?

Do you want to meet the love of your life? Do you want to have a better relationship with your children? Do you want to revitalize your marriage? Do you want to be as fit and energetic as possible? Do you want to do everything you can to be alive and healthy when your great-grandkids come along? Do you want to travel the world, or get a pilot's license, or write a book, or learn a new language? Do you want to own your own business—or your own home? What do you want to do to improve yourself, or help your family and friends?

And as long as you don't get too attached to material possessions, what are some *things* you might want to own? I'm not talking here about status symbols or fancy labels. I'm talking about things you and your family will genuinely enjoy, things that will help you to be playful and have fun, things that won't warp your sense of what's valuable in life—because *all* material possessions are ultimately valueless. If you can adopt the right perspective, if you can own things and not be owned *by* them, then of course it's nice to have a boat, or a beautiful wardrobe of clothes, or a getaway home on some tropical island. Those are all fine goals if you have enough character and humility to handle them.

The second principle of goal setting is that you have to write all these things down and put them in a place where you'll remember to look at them. That's a more important step than you may realize. Most people today don't have written goals at all, and the ones who do usually only look at them once a year—on January 1! Then they put them in a drawer and don't look at them again till the following year. But what if you instead reviewed your goals every single day? Don't you think that would make a big difference in terms of how many of them you end up achieving? Of course it would. Just reading them over at regular intervals will cause you to move toward them. Knowing clearly what you want—and why—will sharpen that inner, subconscious GPS that all of us possess. It will help you to immediately recognize situations and opportunities that might bring you closer to getting what you want.

There's also something in life called "good pressure." It's not the same thing as anxiety, which is always debilitating and useless. Good pressure is when you see that there's a "gap" between where you are now and where you should be in life. Seeing that gap is often the best way to motivate yourself to *close* it. Yes, it's pressure, so it doesn't always feel good—but unlike anxiety, it results in movement and not paralysis.

Imagine for a moment being lost at the bottom of some desolate valley and looking up to the top of a mountain. If the valley was covered with dense clouds and fog, you wouldn't be able to get out. You'd be trapped there. But if it was a bright, sunny day, and you saw the direction you had to go and the distance you had to travel, you could make that journey up the slope to freedom. Writing your goals down and looking at them frequently is the same thing as clearing all that fog out from the valley of your mind. Yes, it's true that the distance you have to go might seem daunting at first, but the *clarity* of mind more than compensates for it. It's what makes the climb possible.

And that brings us to the third and final goal-setting principle: taking action. If you want anything meaningful in life, you have to work at it. God is not about to drop something magnificent into your lap simply because you happen to desire it. He just doesn't do that. Sometimes overly spiritual people think that all they have to do to get what they want is pray for it. But that's nonsense! You have to pray *and* work in order to achieve anything that's worthwhile.

Remember, Jesus Christ didn't save the world just by praying. Sure, he prayed a lot, but he also spent a great deal of his time *acting*. Read the gospels and see if I'm lying! Christ was always healing people, performing miracles, preaching to the crowds, moving here, there, and everywhere. In other words, he was always working. He was always busy "doing his Father's will." And if *he* had to work hard in order to accomplish his objective, then we're going to have to do the same for all our objectives. Doesn't that make sense?

So when you go about setting your goals, you always have to create a list of action steps to go along with them. I can't tell you what those steps should be, because I don't know your goals. I can only tell you to consult with people you trust and people who have already achieved similar goals. I can only tell you to do your research and avoid reinventing the wheel. I can only tell you that you need to take as much action as possible—and that you need to start immediately after you set your goal, in order to build momentum. You've simply got to get that steamroller moving if you're going to overcome all the obstacles that will inevitably be thrown in your path.

Finally, I can only tell you that if you're praying constantly for God's guidance, then that same God is very likely to inspire you with the best possible action steps to take. We've already said that the human soul is made in the image and likeness of God, so when you're in union with him, you're in union with the source of all creative power. You're actually "tapping into" creative genius. A human mind connected to God is really like a giant supercomputer. If the goals you set are in line with what God wants for you, then when you ask him what direction to go, he's going to give you the right answer.

Now I realize it's not always easy to know what God wants. After all, he doesn't exactly hang out signs for us to read. In fact, he sometimes does the opposite. He sometimes plays hide-and-seek with us. He peeks his head out and shows himself, but then quickly darts around the corner and beckons us to follow. When we stop looking for him, he usually comes after us—but even then, he always hides himself for periods of time. That's been God's strategy since time immemorial.

When the apostles Andrew and John first met Jesus, they asked him where he lived. And since Jesus was God in human form, he didn't give them a straight answer! Instead, he just said, "Come and see." He does the same thing with us today. He doesn't give us the crystal-clear certainty we'd like to have. The reason is that he wants us to seek him. He wants us to search for him. He wants us to pray to him. He wants us to follow him. He wants us to do all these things so we can draw into deeper union with him. It's when we're in union with God that we're best able to discern what his will is for us—and for our goals. That's why we always have to include him in all our major planning and decision making. Not only will he help us go in the right direction, but if we start heading down the wrong path, he'll put roadblocks in our way that we *won't* be able to overcome.

That's such an important point to understand. Not every dream you have is God's will for you. In fact, very often your dream is *not* your destiny. Lots of people dream about being artists or actors or musicians—but it's actually the wrong path for them to take. God may have given them a powerful clue about their destiny—but that's just what it was, a *clue*. In order to draw us in closer to him, God leaves it up to us to prayerfully discern the specific goal that his clues point to. He may place in the hearts of certain people the desire to be creative. But whether or not that God-given desire should ultimately be fulfilled through the performing arts, or the visual arts, or the constructive arts, or the medical arts, or any of the other arts in the world, is something God leaves to us to figure out. Many times we can misinterpret God's clues—especially if we're not praying regularly.

Let me tell you a personal story to illustrate what I mean.

From the time I was a little boy I wanted to be a doctor—specifically, a heart surgeon. That's all I wanted to be right up until college. And I might have succeeded, too, if it weren't for a couple of "little" things that got in the way—like organic chemistry, integral calculus, and girls!

When that didn't work out, I felt pretty bad. So I went

back to another great ambition I always had—to be a writer. But I didn't know what kind of writer I wanted to be. I tried everything—political speeches, history textbooks, journalism—but none of it really inspired me. Then, sometime in my twenties, after years of being away from the faith, I started to get more interested in Christianity. There were a lot of reasons for this, but mainly it had to do with some of the books I was reading and some of the people I was meeting. Anyway, I finally started praying to God to lead me in the right direction.

About this time, I took a trip to England and found myself on a train going north from London to Manchester. I had purchased a paperback copy of C. S. Lewis's well-known book *The Screwtape Letters* at the Westminster Abbey bookstore and began reading it as the train pulled out of the station. After just a few pages, I knew I was on to something important. The book made a powerful impression on me. It was the first time I had ever read anything spiritual that made me laugh and think at the same time. It was so cleverly written that I actually read the whole thing from cover to cover and then started over again right after I finished. I'd never done that with any book before.

I had an epiphany on that train ride. I realized that maybe there was a way I could combine *both* of the great ambitions of my life. I realized that maybe God had given me the desire to be a doctor and the desire to be a writer for a reason. If I could write books like *The Screwtape Letters* (not as good, of course), then perhaps I could still have what I always wanted. Perhaps I could still help people who were sick—not with surgery, but with writing.

That was a big revelation to me. For so many years I thought I wanted to be a doctor. But I was wrong. My true desire wasn't to be a doctor at all—it was to be a *healer*. Like many other people, though, I had interpreted the clues God had given me incorrectly. I started to get the right interpretation only when I started to pray.

But that's not the end of the story. It turned out that even having the right interpretation wasn't enough. Ten years later, I *still* hadn't written any spiritual books! The reason was that my vague desire to be a writer was just that—vague. I hadn't really done anything about it. I hadn't created any plan. I hadn't combined my prayer with my God-given common sense and my ability to take action. So in my frustration, I decided to try something new. I decided to employ some rudimentary personal development techniques. Most important, I got serious about goal setting.

It was about this time that I took another train trip—this time from New York to Washington, D.C. I remember it was in the middle of a winter blizzard and I took the slowest train I could find. For close to four hours, all I did was write out my goals. I had a steaming cup of coffee in front of me, and every so often I would look out the window and watch the snow blowing onto the streets and houses as the train sped through the different towns. By the time I arrived in Washington, I had several pages of written goals, together with all my reasons for wanting to achieve them. Even more important, I had put my goals down in a *prayerful* way. Yes, I let my imagination run wild, but I did it with the strong conviction that I wanted to attain these things only if they helped bring me closer to God.

As it turns out, I didn't achieve all the goals I outlined on that train ride. But I did achieve many of them, including the most important one: writing my first book. I decided on that train ride to write *A Travel Guide to Heaven*, and to do it within six months. I looked at my busy workweek, decided which blocks of time I would need to devote to writing, put it on my schedule, and got busy. It was very difficult for me to complete, never having written a book before, and trying to hold down a full-time job at the same time—but with God's help, *I did it*. And it changed my whole life.

You can do it, too! You can achieve whatever goals you set for yourself, no matter how big, as long as God is behind you and you aren't afraid to work hard and pray hard. That's the most effective combination in the world—and that's the combination you need to strive for. Even if you've had experience with goal setting before, it's time to start fresh and try again—this time with an intelligent, written plan and the cooperation of God.

This can be a very important day for you! Be creative. Be daring. Be holy. Find some time to get away for an afternoon and focus on just this subject alone—and then start setting some inspiring goals for yourself!

Believe me, you'll be at the top of that mountain before you even know it.

PART VI

Transform Yourself

"If you're going through hell, keep going."
—Winston Churchill

"Trust in the Lord with all your heart...and he will direct your paths."
—Proverbs 3:5–6

20.

Fighting Evil

We've talked about a lot of topics so far, but do you want to know the truth? You can do everything this book has recommended and still end up being unhappy. That's right. You can learn how to manage your money; you can eat right and exercise; you can live a peaceful, orderly existence; you can be grateful for all the blessings in your life; you can even believe in God and develop a reasonably strong faith—and yet you can still be a frustrated, confused human being.

Why? Because to really get a handle on things, there's something else you have to understand. There's something else you have to take into account as you make your way through the ups and downs of life. It's something the personal development industry never talks about. In fact, it's something many Christians never talk about, either. What is it?

It's called *evil*.

Yes, there is evil in the world. Not just unpleasant things. Not just problems. Not just setbacks. Not just "challenges." Not just "unproductive" ways of dealing with situations. There is evil—real, deadly, diabolical, black-as-night evil.

Self-help experts don't like to talk about that because they don't want to get anybody uncomfortable. They don't want to be viewed as "religious fanatics." They want to appeal to as many people as possible—even those who have completely lost faith in God. So they just don't mention the word *evil*.

But there's a problem with not mentioning it. Even if you ignore evil, it's not going away. And that's why most of these personal development techniques ultimately break down. You can listen to self-help audios all the time and become well versed in the power of positive thinking and make good progress on achieving your goals and believing in yourself—and then one day, when you're least expecting it, evil strikes. Maybe someone you know is raped. Maybe an elderly couple in your neighborhood is brutally attacked. Maybe a little child from the local school is abducted, abused, and murdered by some deviant monster. Evil crimes occur all the time. And when they do, it's pretty hard to focus on the positive. It's pretty hard to believe that your "thoughts" control reality, and that all that's required to "overcome challenges" is to manifest some kind of "positive energy" or "karma." All those easy catchphrases seem so empty in the light of hard, cold, merciless malevolence.

The truth is that you can ignore evil all you want, but evil is *not* going to ignore you. St. Paul said that our struggle in life is not with "flesh and blood" or even the rulers of this world, but rather with "powers and principalities." Do you know what "powers and principalities" are? Those are names for fallen angels—for demons—and for their leader, the devil.

Now, many people in our enlightened culture scoff at the idea of the devil and dismiss any notion of a spiritual world beyond the senses. But if you call yourself a Christian, you're still supposed to believe in those invisible realities. And the reason you're supposed to believe in them is that they're true—they do exist, and they do try to influence people to do bad things.

Like it or not, believe it or not, there's a real spiritual war going on. If you need evidence, just look inside yourself. Look at your own inner battles—all the temptations you have to face on a daily basis—all your dark secrets, all your lusts, all your jealousies, all your grudges, all the little pleasures you sometimes feel when bad things happen to other people. Then look around you. Look at all the terrible evil in the news—the rapes, the killings, the torture, the acts of terrorism, the child molestations, the child pornography, the sadistic violence. Look at the "big" societal evils—the murder rates, the suicide rates, the wars, the genocides. Just look at the abortion rate—twenty million babies killed a year, worldwide. A veritable hemorrhage of blood!

Please don't misunderstand me. I'm not calling anyone in particular evil. Take abortion as an example. God knows that most women who have abortions do so because they feel trapped and pressured by their circumstances and by their families and by their boyfriends. They don't have them because of "freedom of choice," but rather because they feel they have *no freedom* and *no choice*. Of course God has mercy on them. Of course God wants to forgive them. As we've already said in this book, anyone can be forgiven for any sin—no matter how bad—as long as he or she is truly sorry. One tiny drop of Christ's blood is enough to wash away the sins of a billion universes.

But a sin can't be forgiven if you don't think it's a sin. An evil can't be washed away if you insist that it's really a "good." In theology that's what's called a "diabolical inversion." It's when the truth becomes a lie, and a lie becomes the truth. It's what the "powers and principalities" St. Paul spoke of are always working to accomplish. They want a world in which the morality is upside down; in which the positive is negative and the negative is positive.

But let me ask you a question: What happens in life when you do that? What happens when you reverse the polarities of an electric current, for instance—when you switch the charges and make the negative positive? What happens if you do that with the electric wiring in your home? The power gets cut! The lights go out! Darkness envelops everything.

And isn't that exactly the state of our society today? Isn't that exactly the state of so many people's lives? Hasn't the whole moral system been turned on its head? Doesn't spiritual darkness prevail everywhere?

That's one of the main reasons there's so much misery in the world. When darkness prevails on such a large scale, it's almost impossible to be happy—and it doesn't matter what kind of self-help techniques you employ.

The sins that afflict modern society and that afflict each of us, personally, are not just psychological or physical in nature. If they were, we would only need psychological or physical weapons to combat them. But there's a large spiritual component involved. The temptations we face—pride, gluttony, laziness, anger, cruelty, envy, selfishness, infidelity, untruthfulness, despair, etc.—are very real and very strong. And they never let up. Sometimes they seem to take a rest, but not for long. They're always there, trying to act on us in a negative way, trying to pull us down into the slimy gutter, like the force of gravity—heavy, powerful, and relentless.

Personal development tools are wonderful for giving us confidence and teaching us specific ways to schedule our time and achieve our goals, but in the end, they're just not effective at preventing these kinds of temptations from wreaking havoc in our lives. And the reason is that *you can't fight a spiritual battle with worldly weapons.* When you try to do that, the "powers and principalities" sit back and laugh at you! They know that you need to use spiritual weapons for that kind of combat—otherwise you get nowhere.

Christ, himself, said that certain spiritual temptations could only be overcome by "prayer and fasting." He didn't say they could be overcome with positive thinking or with "affirmations" or with written goals or even with the help of support groups—beneficial as those things may be. He said that certain sinful temptations were so powerful and tenacious they could *only* be driven out by prayer and fasting. And if Christ said it, you can be sure it's true.

So let me ask you a question: Do you pray and fast? If not, then you shouldn't complain that you have temptations that are too difficult to resist. The fact is, you're not taking advantage of one of the most important spiritual weapons God gave you to fight evil. Of course you're having trouble with lying or with lust or with rage or with laziness. It makes perfect sense that you can't make progress in overcoming these "hard" sins.

We said earlier that you should pray when you wake up in the morning and before you go to bed at night. And that's very true. But if you've got really serious problems in your life, then you need to be praying a lot more than that. You need to be continually raising your mind to God throughout the course of the day. You need to regularly take the time to find a quiet place and focus just on God. When you start focusing more on God, he'll start focusing more on you and on your problems. Yes, God loves everyone and wants everyone to go to heaven. But God does favors for his friends. He gives the most assistance to those who are closest to him. And the best way to get close to God is to talk to him as much as possible.

Then there's fasting. Everyone forgets about fasting, and yet it's absolutely essential to the spiritual life. Fasting is when you willingly refrain from doing something that's morally permissible because you want to make a sacrifice for God. Usually people refrain from eating for a period of time. And that's probably the best kind of fasting because it directly affects your body. But you can actually fast from anything—music, social media, television, email, shopping—whatever you really enjoy doing. The key is that it's got to be *difficult*. You can't give up something that's easy for you. The whole point is to feel "hungry" and to resist *giving in* to that hunger.

There's just no end to the spiritual benefits of fasting. It disciplines your will. It disciplines your flesh. It strengthens them both far beyond their normal capacity. It literally purifies your body and spirit, and makes it possible for you to pray much more deeply. Remember, all the Old Testament prophets prayed and fasted. Jesus prayed and fasted. His disciples prayed and fasted. The early church prayed and fasted. And great Christians down through the ages have prayed and fasted. There's a reason they did it—*it works*. And if it worked for them, it can work for you.

Let me ask you another question: Do you attend church regularly—or are you one of those people who think that's not important? If you're part of the latter group, then you're really missing out on one of the most powerful spiritual weapons that God has given to us to fight evil. I talked about this in another book I wrote, *Angels All Around Us*. I said that to be a Christian means that you're part of a family. When Jesus taught people to pray, he didn't tell them to say, "*My* Father, who art in heaven"; he told them to say, "*Our* Father." And he also said to his disciples, "When *two or three* gather together in my name—I shall be there among them."

Believing in God is not strictly a one-on-one affair. It involves everyone. It involves the whole community of believers. Having a personal relationship with the Lord—which is something everyone needs—is never an excuse for self-absorption, self-centeredness, and isolation. As we noted earlier in this book, it's no accident that the symbol of our faith isn't a circle or some other closed figure, but rather a cross, with its beams extending outward in all directions—north, south, east, and west. To be a Christian, by definition, means to go *out* of yourself, and not just to retreat inward.

I know it can be difficult sometimes to go to church. It can be tedious. It can be boring. It's so much easier to do it "all by yourself." Catholics are probably the worst offenders when it comes to this. I know because I happen to be one. Catholics say they believe in the "real presence" of Christ in the Eucharist, and then they hardly ever go to Mass—even on Sundays. Catholics say they believe in seven sacraments (most Christians have two or three) and yet they rarely take advantage of any of them. Catholics say they've been given the "fullness of truth," and yet most of them think they can just pick and choose whatever doctrines of the faith appeal to them—and reject the ones they don't like. Then they complain that Christian morality is too difficult to practice!

Too difficult to practice? Of course it's too difficult to practice! In fact it's impossible to practice the way they do it and as so many other Christians do it. How in the world can you hope to follow the moral teaching of Jesus Christ in this secular, hedonistic age without ever getting any spiritual nourishment from Jesus Christ? It's like trying to defeat an enemy when you've got both hands tied behind your back. To quote Chesterton again, "It's not that the

Christian ideal has been tried and found wanting. It's that it's been found difficult and left untried!"

St. Paul said it a different way. In a famous passage from his letter to the Ephesians, he warned believers about the need to *"put on the full armor of God... so that when the day of evil comes, you may be able to stand your ground."*

Notice that he said the *full* armor of God. Not some of the armor. Not a piece of the armor. But all of it. Every last bit of it. The reason he said that is that the devil is a good shot! If you have big holes in your defenses, you're going to get hit—and you're going to fall.

Don't make that mistake. Don't spend decades amassing money and friends and reputation and power and personal development skills in an attempt to secure happiness, and then forget that evil can wipe it all out in the blink of an eye. Don't be so naïve to think you're safe and secure—because you're not. Nobody is.

Instead, be intelligent—spiritually intelligent. Find some good books on spiritual combat and study them. Pray and fast regularly, especially during times of great temptation. Read the Bible, not just once in a while, but all the time. Worship and take the sacraments with your fellow believers—don't be arrogant and try to do it by yourself. Above all, learn your faith, increase your faith, and be sure that God is the center of your life.

If you use these and other spiritual weapons, then when

that day of evil comes, you'll be able to stand your ground without wavering, just as St. Paul promised. You'll be able to be happy even in the midst of the worst trials. Indeed, you'll be able to *overcome* the worst trials. And if you persevere in using these weapons, I guarantee that no matter how deep the darkness that surrounds you, your light will always shine forth and serve as a powerful beacon to your family and your friends and all who know you.

That's a heck of a lot more than any kind of positive thinking will ever do for you.

21.

Strength in the Midst of Suffering

In the previous chapter we talked about evil. In this chapter we're going to talk about suffering. I know it's not a lot of fun reading about these subjects. Believe me, it's even less fun to write about them. But I really want this book to give you a whole program for life, and in order to do that, I have to include those things that make life so hard and so painful so much of the time.

I also want to be fair. I've taken a few shots at the personal development industry in this book, but when it comes to dealing with much of the frustration and depression we experience on a daily basis, self-help programs can actually be quite effective. For example, I've learned some important things from the work of Tony Robbins—things that have helped shape who I am and inspired me to get back on track when I've been in a rut; things that have showed me how to stay positive when I've felt over-whelmed by problems.

It's not always easy to do that. The human brain seems to gravitate to the negative. In fact I know a lot of people who specialize in being pessimistic. You meet them for breakfast or lunch, and within five minutes they've com-plained about everything from the slow service to the light-ing in the room to the problems in the Middle East. They just zero in like laser beams on everything that's wrong with the world. Their focus is always negative, and then they wonder why they're miserable.

The self-help industry helped me realize the importance of disciplining my thinking so I could more easily focus on the positive—even when I was "feeling" negative. Being a full-blooded Italian and passionate by nature, it's never been difficult for my "temperature" to rise. And living in New York City has not exactly been a calming influence. When stressful situations occur, it's easy to slip into a com-plaining, self-pitying mode. It's easy to say things like "Why does this always happen to me?"

But by constant practice and self-discipline, I've learned to make the most of stressful situations by asking myself better questions, like "What can I learn from this prob-lem?" or "What can I do now that will motivate me and give me some hope?" or "Despite this challenge, what am I grateful for?" I've discovered that it's much simpler to be happy when you're able to control your thinking process; when you're able train your mind to resist the pull of emotional gravity; when you're able to finally break the "habit" of negative thinking.

Regarding problem solving, one of the best lessons I learned is to spend no more than twenty percent of my time thinking about the problems themselves. The other eighty percent has to be devoted to trying to figure out their solution. Usually people do the reverse, don't they? They dwell too much on the details of their problems. They play the "tape" of their troubles over and over again in their minds until they work themselves up into a state of black depression. And once they're in that state, it's hard for them to get out of it. Usually they end up taking the easy route of *temporarily* relieving their pain by doing things that aren't always good for them—physically, mentally, or spiritually. What they don't realize is that it's a lot more effective to spend your time fixing your problems, instead of fixating on them. Yes, it takes a certain kind of mental discipline to do that, but it's possible—and the self-help industry is good at teaching it.

But then there are problems that no personal development technique in the world can remedy. And this is where Christianity comes into play again, because Christianity teaches that while it's possible to be joyful under any circumstances, life on this earth will always be a "vale of tears and a place of trial." To deny that is to deny reality itself. To live is to suffer—sometimes, to suffer intensely. And when intense suffering comes—whether it's grieving over the loss of someone you love, or the fear of that kind of loss—there's only one thing that really works: *total abandonment to the will of God.*

What you have to understand is that nothing happens in the universe unless God either wills it or allows it to happen. Nothing happens to *you* unless God wills it or allows it to happen. Nothing in life occurs by chance, nothing is an accident, nothing is a coincidence.

That doesn't mean that God *wants* tragic things to take place—like car accidents or diseases or terrorist attacks. God isn't some sadistic witch doctor poking pins in his human puppets in order to cause them pain. He would much rather that our lives be free from suffering. But the fact is, he's chosen to create a world in which free will prevails—a world in which evil and suffering can occur. And he permits it only because he knows that someday, in some way, by the mysterious workings of his divine providence, he's going to pull some greater good out of it.

Therefore, you have to accept on faith that everything in life—whether it's wealth, poverty, sickness, health, blessings, or trials—comes from the hand of God, and ultimately is for the benefit of your immortal soul.

Now it's important to be careful here. Abandonment to

God's will isn't to be confused with fatalism or quietism or cowardice. Just because God is in charge doesn't mean that you sit back and do nothing when action is called for. Quite the contrary. If a problem arises, you have to deal with it. If you're sick, you have to call the doctor. If you're in legal trouble, you have to call a lawyer. If you see an injustice, you have to fight it. God expects you to do everything that needs to be done in order to solve your problem. But once you're finished, you have to let it go. You have to relinquish it. You have to try your best to be at peace—to know in the deepest part of your soul that God is in control. If, despite your best efforts, all your hopes and dreams seem to be dashed, you have to accept that as part of God's plan for you.

Is that always easy to do? Of course not! As I've said so often in this book, it's sometimes impossible to control your feelings, even on an hour-to-hour basis. But abandonment isn't about feelings. It's about your will. When you see yourself worrying about a problem, when you see the anxiety and fear starting to build inside you, that's the time to make a conscious effort to take a breath, recollect yourself, and say with confidence, "I know you're here with me, God. I know you're watching over me. I know this is your will. I know that nothing happens without your permission." So while your emotions may revolt and even tremble, your will can still be at peace and say, "No, I will not be afraid."

Unfortunately, there may be times when even doing that seems impossible; times when you're deathly afraid that something terrible might happen, something like financial ruin, or the breakup of your marriage, or cancer; times when you literally find it difficult to breathe, when your whole body goes limp, when your knees start to buckle and the only thing you want to do is collapse somewhere—anywhere—and close your eyes and shut out the whole world.

In those dark days of radical fear, radical abandonment is the *only* answer. Christ said in the gospels, "Fear is useless. What is necessary is trust." When he said that, he was speaking as God Almighty, and he was speaking for all times and for all situations.

The simple fact is that the more you trust God, the more he'll help you get through whatever crisis you're experiencing. He may not perform any miracles for you or take away the crisis itself, but he'll always get you through the storm with your faith and peace of mind intact. No matter how great your fear, you just have to keep saying, "Jesus, I trust in you." It doesn't matter if you say it a million times. You just have to say it over and over again, out loud and to yourself, morning, noon, and night, as you drift off to sleep, and as you wake up. You have to make it part of your very breathing.

Now, if someone close to you has already died, you

might have to do a few other things to make it through the searing pain as well.

Not only do you have to trust that God has a plan for you, but you also have to trust that time really does heal all wounds. It may take years, but the pain *will* eventually subside. At the very least, it will be dulled. The important thing to understand is that people heal in their own ways and at their own rates. Don't ever let anyone tell you differently. If some well-meaning friends think you've been grieving too long and that it's time to "move on," then it's the time to politely tell *them* to move on—to some other topic of conversation.

Then there's that old saying about the healing power of salt. Have you ever heard it? "Salt is the remedy for all suffering," it's been said. And I've found it to be very true. Not table salt, of course. But salt from the sweat of hard work, salt from the tears of crying, and salt that comes from being near or on the sea. Those three things always seem to act as a soothing balm for the wounded soul.

And finally, if none of that works, you can try one other remedy: you can try thinking long and hard about a place called heaven. People today just don't think about heaven enough. I've written an adult book and a children's book on the subject because I don't believe there's anything more important in the spiritual life to pray about or meditate about. If people meditated about heaven for five minutes a day, their lives would be completely transformed.

The Bible says that "eye has not seen, nor ear heard, nor have entered into the heart of man, the things that God has prepared for those who love him." So many people today forget that. They picture heaven as some bright, beautiful place filled with puffy clouds and cartoonish figures of angels wearing long white robes. The images they have in their minds are so unclear and overly spiritualized that it's no wonder they're not more excited by the idea of going there someday.

But that's not what Christianity teaches about heaven at all. Christianity teaches that if the world we're living in now is real, then heaven is not going to be less real than that. It's going to be *more* real—more colorful, more dynamic, more adventurous, more creative, more filled with passion, more filled with energy, more filled with relationships, more filled with love.

And after the Resurrection, heaven isn't just going to be a spiritual place; it's going to be *physical*, too. That means that when you see your mother or father or sister or brother or son or daughter again, you won't just be seeing an unrecognizable ghost. You'll be seeing *them*—their whole person—body and soul. You'll be able to run up to them and hug them and kiss them and look into their eyes and feel the warmth of their skin and talk to them and hear their voice again—the same way you did when they were alive. Only the love you share with them will be deeper than ever before and completely untainted by all the petty jealousies and animosities and grudges that constantly plague our relationships here on earth.

The main thing to grasp is this: If you've lost a relative or a friend and that person is with God, then they're doing just fine. They're okay. They're happier than they've ever been before. In fact, they're doing much better than you and I. All they've really done is moved homes. They've "relocated" to God's home—heaven—and they're waiting for us to get there, too.

Listen, life is ridiculously short. It goes by in the "blink of an eye." No matter what age you live to, it's really just a drop of water in the ocean of eternity. If you've lost a child or a teenager, please remember that. Remember that a person who dies young has just gotten something over with that all of us have to go through eventually. Yes, what happened to them is terrible and tragic, but at least they're done with the toughest part of life—the "dying" part. We still have to do it. And while having a good time can be a wonderful thing, having it ten times more by living longer doesn't make it any better. The only thing that counts—and I mean the *only* thing—is getting to heaven. If you die at ten years old in an automobile accident and become a saint in heaven, then you've had a magnificent life. But if you die at one hundred, rich and powerful in the eyes of the world, but go to hell, then your life was a miserable, wasted failure.

You've got to believe that—not because of any self-help principles, but because it's *true*. You can read hundreds of spiritual books on grieving and suffering, and they're all going to tell you the same thing. They're all going to say that God has a plan that you can't always see—but it's one you always have to trust in. Everything comes down to trust in God.

Can you do that? Can you "let go and let God"?

Can you relinquish all your anxiety to him, and trust that he'll provide you with everything you need in life, in a time and a place and a manner best suited to your own soul?

I'm telling you that you're never going to be able to be happy in this world unless you try. There's just too much pain to bear. You can't shoulder it alone. You're not strong enough. No one is. No matter how much money or confidence or knowledge or power you possess, you're still just a little boat being tossed about on the waves of a stormy sea. At some point, those waves are going to come crashing down on you.

When that happens—when the world becomes just too much of a burden for you—there's only one thing to do. You have to give all your fear and dread and doubt and grief and pain to the One who said, *"Be of good cheer, for I have overcome the world."*

When you do that, when you totally abandon yourself to God's divine will, he will give you a happiness that transcends all worldly understanding, because it's not from this world. Rather, it's a foretaste of the supreme happiness God wants you to enjoy forever—in heaven.

22.

All You Need Is Love?

Everyone seems to think that the most important thing you need to be happy in life is love.

Isn't that what the millions of love songs and romance novels and poems and movies and TV shows all say? Isn't that the one thing that liberals and conservatives, modernists and traditionalists, atheists and believers, Christians and Jews, all agree on? Back in the 1960s the Beatles sang, "All you need is love." But didn't the Bible say the same thing more than two thousand years ago? Didn't St. Paul say that only three things last forever: faith, hope, and love—and that "the greatest of these is love"? And didn't the gospels themselves say that "God is love"?

Well, if popular culture and the Bible both agree—and they don't agree on much of anything—that's pretty good evidence that something might be true. And yet, if it really is the case that love is all you need to be happy, why does everyone seem to be so unhappy? If everyone knows the right medicine to take, why are they still so sick?

I'll tell you the answer. It's not that the medicine is at fault. It's actually one hundred percent effective. Love *is* all you need. The problem is that the definition everybody is using for the word "love" is incorrect. The problem is that we have our labels screwed up again.

We talked earlier in this book about how using the wrong label on a map might make you go in the wrong direction and end up in the wrong place. But what if you switched labels on medicine bottles? What if you thought you were taking aspirin but it was really some kind of hallucinogenic drug? What if you thought you were taking the cure to a disease, but it was really poison?

That's exactly what we've done today with love. We've switched labels on the medicine bottle and people are swallowing all kinds of "pills" that pass for love but are actually quite harmful—especially if taken at the wrong times or in the wrong combinations or in the wrong doses.

Take "infatuation," for example. Many people mistakenly label that love. And it's understandable. After all, is there any greater feeling in the world than having a "crush" on someone? Is there anything better than having those fluttering butterflies in your stomach? That ache in your heart? Those obsessive thoughts flying around your head? If

you've ever been lucky enough to feel that way about someone and then have those feelings reciprocated, you know
what a special and magical thing it can be.

And yet, is infatuation love? Is that really what the
gospels describe as being *equal* to God? Is it even what the
Beatles song is about? Is it all you need to be happy? I don't
think so. In fact, if you mislabel infatuation as love, you had
better be very careful, because at the wrong time and place,
that wonderful, beautiful feeling could actually be highly
toxic.

Don't believe me? What happens if you've been married
fifteen years and have three kids and you suddenly get infatuated with a coworker? What happens if you further mistake that feeling of infatuation for love? Is there a chance
you might do something stupid and wreck your marriage?
Is there a chance you might do tremendous damage to your
children? Is there a chance you might ruin your career? If
you indulge your desires and give in to your feelings, do
you really think that qualifies as love, or is it just a sign of
immaturity—and selfishness?

Listen, gasoline is a great invention and it's what your
car needs to function well and take you to nice places,
but if you ever drink a gallon of it, you'll end up in the
hospital real quick. Likewise, infatuation can be a delicious treat to sample if you're not married and if the
person you're infatuated with is single and likes you, too.

But if that's not the situation, don't go confusing it for love—because a few too many bites of that treat might be enough to give you a case of food poisoning that could wipe you out.

Or take another example: kindness. Many people mistake kindness for love, too. Kindness is when you try to alleviate someone else's suffering. After all, nobody likes suffering. We all want to eliminate it forever. It hurts for us to see people in pain—especially if we love them. And yet, isn't pain good for us sometimes? Doesn't it help us to grow? Doesn't it help us to mature? Doesn't it even, on occasion, lead us to happiness? And so isn't it sometimes an act of true love to allow or even cause someone to experience a certain amount of pain?

Come on, you know it's true. A few chapters ago we talked about spoiled children and how they become that way. There's probably no better example of love that's been mislabeled. When a child cries and screams because he doesn't want to go to the doctor or the dentist or to school, it's so easy to give in to him. We don't want to see him cry. We want to be kind to him. We want him to laugh and play and give us lots of kisses. But is it really loving for us to do that? What happens to that child if he doesn't go through the pain he's supposed to?

I'll tell you what happens. If he doesn't go to the doctor he's going to get sick. If he doesn't go to the dentist his teeth will rot and fall out. If he doesn't go to school he's going to stay ignorant and never go anywhere in life. In other words, he's going to experience *real* suffering later on—and it's going to be *your* fault because of your well-meaning but misguided attempt to be kind when you should have been firm.

The point is that kindness, like infatuation, isn't genuine love at all. It's just one aspect of love. Under the wrong circumstances it can be disastrous to a person.

So what *is* the correct label for love? How can we understand it in a way that it will be good for us at all times and in all amounts? This is one of the key questions in life, isn't it? If we answer it correctly, it will really put us on the right road to peace and happiness. And yet, this is where I have to warn you that if you embark on a journey to discover love's true meaning, it's going to take you away from the world of pop culture, with all its phony, silly, shallow clichés. It's going to take you far out of your comfort zone and into some very dangerous territory. It's going to take you to a place where your spiritual, emotional, and physical strength is tested to the limit. It's going to take you right up to the cross.

Yes, the cross—the greatest symbol of love in the universe. The cross, because that's what love is ultimately about: self-sacrifice, self-denial, and self-giving—even to the point of death.

True love cares about what's *best* for the other person. Not just what feels good. Not just what gives you butterflies in your stomach. Not just what gets you sexually aroused. Not just what alleviates pain. True love is so much more than all that. True love suffers. It sacrifices. It gives till it hurts. But if you practice it, you'll find that it really is a cure-all for life's problems. And the reason is that true love *is* the substance of God. It is magnificent and profound and sublime and, truth be told, almost never soft. In fact, it's incredibly hard. So hard that some have even compared it to a rock—the rock on which Christ founded his church.

But in order to understand this kind of love, you first need to understand something else—and it's very important that we don't skip over it. To understand love, you have to understand life, too. Both are tied together inextricably, and any attempt to fathom one without the other is doomed to failure.

Of course, everyone nowadays seems to make a big deal over what a "mystery" life is. So many modern philosophers and writers and filmmakers have tried to discover its meaning but have come up short. In fact, their conclusion has been that the search itself is endless and hopeless and even pointless. But guess what? I can tell you all you need to know about the meaning of life in one short sentence:

For God so loved the world that he gave his one
and only Son, that whoever believes in him shall
not perish but have eternal life. (John 3:16)

That's it. That's the "secret" of life. It may not spell out
the details, but all the main points are there.

First, there is a God. A personal God. And he loves us.

Second, Jesus Christ *is* God—God the son, God the
second person of the Blessed Trinity, God in human form.

Third, God became a man for one reason—to save us
from our sins. Christians believe that God lowered himself
and took on our human nature so that we could be raised up
and share in his higher, divine nature. That's what "redemption" is all about. After the disobedience of our first parents
in the Garden of Eden, human beings weren't allowed to
enter heaven. But through a life of total obedience—even
to the point of self-sacrifice on the cross—Christ made up
for the original sin of our first parents, redeemed our fallen
human nature, reconciled us to God, and opened the gates
of heaven to us. Christ's mission was the salvation of the
world.

And *our* mission is to enter into that salvation—to enter
into the life and work of Christ himself, by imitating him,
by uniting ourselves to his body, and by becoming what
C. S. Lewis called "little Christs." That's the meaning and
purpose of life on this planet, and nothing else.

Do you see why life and love are so closely connected? Their purpose is exactly the same—to give, to sacrifice, to be Christlike, to be in union with God.

Now, I know that all this might seem a lot to get your mind around. It is. And if this were a book of Christian apologetics, I would probably spend several chapters giving you all the reasons and explanations and arguments why Christians believe what they do. But this isn't a book of Christian apologetics. It's a "how-to" book on transforming your life and finding true happiness. The "proof" for this book isn't in its arguments, but in the *results* you get.

And the results you get from true love are nothing short of miraculous. In fact, they're enough to transform your marriage, your family, your career, and the entire fabric of your existence. But growing in love is an extremely difficult process. It takes time and effort and practice. Like old age, it's not for sissies.

After all, if you want to grow in anything in life, you have to exercise hard, right? "No pain, no gain" is a very true saying. If you want your body to get stronger, you have to exercise it by working out. If you want your memory to improve, you have to exercise it by trying to recall things. If you want to get better at playing a musical instrument, you have to exercise by practicing every day.

Well, it's the same with the spiritual life—especially when it comes to love. If you want to grow in it, you have to exercise by *loving more*. You have to exercise by testing your willingness to give, give, and give some more. And that's exactly what God does to us all the time. He pushes us to our limits. He sends us trials that force us to grow. God is the greatest—and toughest—coach in the world. If you ask him to increase your faith and your love, don't be surprised if he responds by making life very hard for you—at first.

Did you ever hear the story about the great Spanish mystic Teresa of Avila? She was an extremely holy woman and was always praying to God to increase her faith and love. Once she was traveling somewhere in the countryside during the winter and got caught in a storm. It was the dead of night and there was lightning and thunder and wind and her horse and wagon went off the side of the road and dumped her into a ditch full of mud. As she was struggling to climb out in the pouring rain, she couldn't resist looking up at the dark sky and yelling, "Oh Lord, if this is the way you treat your friends, it's no wonder you have so few of them!"

Don't you ever feel that way sometimes? I know I do. It's natural. But the question is, if God loved Teresa of Avila, what motive did he have for treating her that way? He knew she was holy. He knew she was "one of his friends." Yet he was so rough on her. Why? The simple reason is that he was answering her prayer. He was giving her the opportunity to work on her faith and her love. He knew that the only way he could help her to become stronger was to challenge her, to push her to her limits, to exercise her.

And if he did it to her, you can be sure he'll do it to you, too! So instead of railing at God when he sends you trials, why not just get down to the hard work of increasing your love?

Do you ever do that? Do you ever actually work on improving your capacity to love? Do you work at loving yourself, for instance? Do you take care of your body and your soul by nourishing them properly and by developing your willpower? Or do you just spoil yourself? Do you simply give in to your body every time it calls out for food, or rest, or comfort, or sexual gratification? If you're not practicing self-control, you're just becoming a slave to your flesh. And that's not love.

What about your neighbors? Do you work at loving them—starting with your family? Do you love them, even to the point of death? Christ didn't just give part of himself to the world. He gave every last drop of blood. Do you do that for your spouse and children? Or do you spend a lot of time whining about how difficult you have it and how ungrateful they are?

What about acquaintances and strangers? Do you practice hospitality—even to people you don't like? Remember, loving isn't the same as liking. "Liking" is purely an emotion. Love isn't. You can dislike a person intensely but still be kind to them, pray for them, and sacrifice for them. In fact, the people you dislike most in life are sometimes the ones God expects you to show the greatest love toward.

How about charity? Do you give generously, not just out of your abundance but out of your need? Do you give without expecting anything back—not even credit or recognition? I'll tell you something: If you're looking for reciprocation of any kind, then it's no longer true love you're practicing, but just another form of selfishness. Yes, you might be accomplishing some good with your charitable gifts, but if you're anxiously waiting for payback, that only makes it a more "refined," "sophisticated" type of selfishness. True love doesn't ever expect to be "rewarded" in this life. In fact, it's more likely to be ignored, neglected, abandoned, or punished—just as Christ was when he was hanging on the cross.

Finally, what about God, himself? Do you work at loving him—or do you just give him lip service? Do you thank him every day? Do you praise him? Do you worship him—not just at home but at church? Do you try to obey his commandments—not some of them, but all of them? When you fall, do you confess your sins and repent? And when he sends you trials, do you turn tail and run from them? Or do you instead say, "Lord, thank you for counting me *worthy* to share in a small part of your cross. Help me to carry it so I can use it to honor you and give you glory"?

That's true love.

You have to get it through your head that the cross isn't something negative—it's something positive. In fact, if you look closely at it, you'll see that it's actually a huge "plus sign." We talked a few chapters ago about fighting evil. Do you know that the best, most effective spiritual weapon there is to combat evil is redemptive love—love that has been united to the suffering of Christ? When you love people so much that it hurts, it puts you at the very pinnacle of spiritual power. It unites you to the source of power itself— Jesus Christ—at the very moment he demonstrated his saving power to humanity.

When you give without limit, you "plug in" to that power source—and it begins to have a transformational effect on everything you do. When you love the people in your family that way—no matter how ungrateful they may be—your family life begins to transform. When you love the people at your work that way—no matter how irritating they may be—your work environment begins to transform. When you practice the kind of love Jesus taught on the cross, you yourself begin to transform into the best father, mother, husband, wife, son, daughter, friend, employer, co-worker possible.

But talk is cheap. *Talk is cheap!* You don't bring about that kind of radical transformation by singing Beatles songs. You do it with radical action! You do it by praying and working at it every single day of your life. You do it by getting off your butt and helping people who are suffering. You do it by giving every last drop of blood to your family and your friends and your town and your city and your country and your world. You do it by constantly exercising your love, by sacrificing your wants and needs for the sake of others. You do it by uniting yourself to the cross.

When you live *that* way—as a Christian is really called to live—then yes, it's true, love is all you need.

23.

All This, and Heaven, Too!

The moral of this book can be summed up in one line
from the Psalms:

> *If the Lord does not build the house, then the*
> *builders labor in vain.*

So many people today try to "build" their own lives and
give no heed whatsoever to the kind of life God wants for
them. The end result is that we have a world brimming over
with unhappy people.

No one ever seems to learn. So many folks are content
to spend the precious few years they have on this planet trying to get more money so they can show off. They might
not admit it, but that's the truth. They don't want to buy a
house they really love; they want one that looks fancier and

makes them appear richer. The same goes for their cars and their clothes and their furniture and all the rest of their possessions. It's all about showing off. It's all about status.

How pathetic! The misguided masses that get caught up in the battle over expensive labels and shiny status symbols just don't realize what a waste of time it is. They don't realize what a waste of *life* it is. Who do they think they're showing off for? Who are they trying to impress? What's the point? Do they really think that other people look at them and say, "Wow, John's doing great. He's so rich and successful. I admire John." Are they really silly enough to believe that?

The irony is that people aren't thinking about "John" at all. They're too busy thinking about themselves! And if they did give him and his possessions a passing thought, it would probably be in a disparaging way. That's just how people are today. They don't view their neighbors' accomplishments with charity and humility—they view them in a spirit of competition; they view them enviously.

It's all a big waste of time. It's all a silly rat race. And as someone very wise once said, the outcome of that race doesn't matter much, because even if you win, you're still a rat!

Is that what you want to be in life? A rat?

The same holds true for people who lust for power. So many of them don't realize that their huge ambition to

become "important" and "powerful" is really just a manifestation of their huge ego and insecurity complex. Any
worldly position, no matter how lofty, is insignificant in
the grand scheme of things. Even the job of president of
the United States is grossly overrated. Outside of our own
country, being president just isn't a big deal. Nobody cares
very much how "powerful" he is. In fact, if the president
took a leisurely stroll down the Via Veneto in Rome, he
wouldn't even need a security detail. Not one Italian would
bother looking up from his newspaper and espresso. The
truth is that people who run for elective office because
they think it's going to make them "important" are just
kidding themselves. Worldly importance is purely a local
phenomenon.

Even those rare individuals who achieve great, international fame are usually forgotten within a couple of
generations. If you want proof, just take a trip to England,
France, or Italy and walk through some of the ancient
churches and palaces. You'll see hundreds—even thousands—of marble busts of past monarchs. Nobody even
knows who these people are now because time has erased
and eroded the names that were carved into the stone.
And these were the kings of the world! These were the
richest, most powerful men and women of their time. They
went to their graves certain in the knowledge that they had
secured some measure of lasting fame, that they had really

done something *special* in their lives; that they would be remembered.

But they were all wrong. Dead wrong. It was just vanity.

Do you get my point? You have to forget about impressing the people around you. You have to forget about impressing posterity. You have to stop living a life of worthless delusion. It's all a load of horse manure! The only one you have to worry about impressing is God Almighty. The reputation and standing you have in *his* eyes is the only reputation and standing that counts. *He's* the only one who can give you happiness in this life and the world to come—and no one else.

Let's take a moment now to talk about "happiness." We've mentioned that word so many times in these pages, but we haven't really discussed it at length. Let's do that right now and let's be *honest* about it.

The truth is that it's possible to be happy in this life, but you can't ever be *perfectly* happy. If you do all the things this book recommends, I'm sure that you'll be *very* happy. I'm sure you'll experience a state of supreme contentment, joy, and tranquility—one that won't ever be disturbed by the ups and downs of life. As the Bible says, it will be so marvelous it will "transcend all understanding." But don't kid yourself. It *still* won't be perfect. It still won't be complete.

That's the bottom line, and we might as well face it once and for all. I don't care what religion you practice, what belief system you adopt, what method of positive thinking you employ, or what personal development program you follow. None of those things will ever give you perfect happiness. That's because perfect happiness isn't something you can get from any activity or created thing. It certainly isn't something you can get from the pleasures of this world—not even if you have a lifetime of them.

You know this is true! Haven't there been times in your life when you obtained something you once thought would make you happy—but when you finally got it, it didn't produce the effect you desired? Maybe you always wanted a trip to Paris, or you always wanted a boat, or you always wanted to get married, or you always wanted to be wealthy. When you finally got those things they gave you *some* happiness, yes, but none of them made you completely happy. None of them gave you what you were really looking for. That's because "pleasures are always greater in the anticipation than they are in the realization."

In fact, having lots of pleasures can even dull your ability to be satisfied. C. S. Lewis said that the whole lesson of his life was that no method of stimulation was of any lasting use. "They're all like drugs," he said. "A stronger dose is needed each time and soon no dose is effective."

That's why the hedonists of the world are such a pitiful lot. They spend their whole lives chasing mirages—false visions of things they think will make them happy but never do. Then, after they've been disappointed for the thousandth time, they get frustrated and disillusioned and turn into cynics. They end up becoming the loudest of complainers, blaming everyone and everything for their problems—except themselves. They say things like "It's my wife's fault" or "It's my parents' fault" or "It's my boss's fault" or "It's the president's fault"—all because none of those people ever did what they were supposed to do. They never provided perfect happiness.

But who's to blame for that? Christianity has taught for centuries that true, perfect happiness comes from God alone. It's something we'll be able to experience only in heaven, when we see God face-to-face.

Ultimately, any unhappiness we experience in life isn't due to a lack of fame or fortune or high position. It's due to a lack of something inside *us*. Human beings were created by God with immortal souls—and those souls can't be satisfied by mere earthly pleasures. Fulton Sheen once said that if the sun could speak, it would say it was happy when it was shining, and if a pencil could speak, it would say it was happy when it was writing—because those are the purposes for which they were made.

Well, *we* were made for the purpose of being in full union with God in heaven, and anything short of that—including the greatest pleasures of this world—is doomed to disappoint us.

What you have to understand is that the pleasures we derive from beautiful, good, and true things on earth are just *reflections* of God himself, who is *infinite* beauty, goodness, and truth. Sometimes, at very rare moments, we're lucky enough to get a glimpse of what our happiness in heaven is going to be like—perhaps when we hear a moving piece of music, or when we see a spectacular wonder of nature, or when we're in love, or when we witness some heroic act of courage and self-sacrifice. Usually those experiences are all too fleeting and strike us in such a profound way that they're beyond words. But in reality, those moments are actually a preview of what heaven is going to be like *all the time*.

That's a wonderful thing to look forward to. And knowing that imperfect happiness is the only kind we're ever going to have on earth isn't necessarily a bad thing, either. In fact, it's a blessing. It means you don't have to be disappointed every time a great experience leaves you feeling unfulfilled. It means you don't have to waste your time searching for any utopias that don't exist. It means you can concentrate on what's really important—making sure you get to heaven at the end of your days, and enjoying the gift of life as much as possible now.

But for the last time, you can't sit still and wait for that joy to be given to you! It's just not going to happen. One of the key teachings of Christianity is that if you want anything in life, you have to first work on *yourself*. Self-improvement always precedes great accomplishment—and that includes the accomplishment of great happiness.

People are always batting their brains out trying to change their circumstances or change the behavior of the people around them. But that approach rarely works—so why not just forget it altogether? If you want a better family life, work on becoming the best, kindest, strongest family man possible. If you want to rise in your career, work on becoming the best, most valuable employee possible. In other words, if you want to attract people, work on becoming attractive yourself—not just physically but in every way. Hemingway once said that if you really do good work and grow creatively, other people will be attracted to you, "as surely as migrating birds are drawn at night to a powerful beacon."

Work on becoming a beacon, and you'll be amazed at how many wonderful things in life come your way!

That applies to the spiritual life, too. No great person who reformed the world ever started out by trying to reform the world. They always began by trying to reform themselves first. Only after they achieved some level of self-mastery did God use them in a powerful way to effect lasting change. And doesn't that make sense? If God—the author of life—wants to "write" something important in the history of the world, don't you think he'd prefer to use the best writing instrument possible? Yes, it's true that he sometimes uses sinners to accomplish his will—because God can "draw straight lines with crooked pencils"—but he always sharpens those pencils very quickly. He always turns great sinners into great saints.

That's the course you have to set for yourself—to become a great saint. Remember, the only definitive failure in life is the failure to become a saint, the failure to go to heaven.

Is it hard work? Of course it is! But it's joyful work, too. And you can do it. You just have to change your perspective. You just have to put into practice some of the things we've talked about in this book. You have to grow in your relationship with God through prayer and the life of his church; you have to abandon yourself to his holy will; you have to try to obey all his teachings and commandments; you have to exercise true love toward your neighbor; you have to take up your cross every day and unite it to the sufferings of Christ. Those are the things you have to do in order to grow in closer union with God—and those are the things that will give you a foretaste of the happiness of heaven, *right now*.

It doesn't matter if you've been a "bad" Christian up to this point. It doesn't matter if you've been the worst sinner in the world. You have an immortal, everlasting soul, made in the image and likeness of God. That means you have superhuman power to completely change your life at any moment you decide.

Listen, when Jesus Christ rose from the dead that first Easter Sunday, who was the first person he appeared to? It wasn't St. Peter. It wasn't St. Paul. It wasn't any of the other apostles. It was Mary Magdalene, a former prostitute!

Did you ever realize that? At the most important moment in all history, God Almighty—the God of Life, the God of Love, the God of Power, the God of Creation—chose to appear to a *prostitute* before revealing himself to anyone else. Do you think that was an accident? It wasn't! There *are* no accidents in Sacred Scripture. God was making a very specific point. He was saying that you can start out as the greatest sinner in the world and still end up being *first* in the Kingdom of Heaven.

Once and for all, forget about your past! None of that means anything. The only thing that counts is what you do going forward. The only thing that counts is how you live the rest of your life. And *please*, don't ever be envious of anybody. Don't waste your time with fantasies about how wonderful it would be to switch places with some billionaire or president or rock star or sports star or movie star. Those are all nice things to do, but they're all beneath you. *Beneath* you!

You've been given the highest, most magnificent vocation there is in life. It's called being a Christian! Live up to that vocation—*really* live up to it, not just with words but with actions; with every ounce of strength you can muster.

I promise that if you do, you'll have all the love, peace, and joy that this world has to offer—and heaven, too.

God bless you!

A Rainy Walk in the Eternal City

"I believe in Christianity the way I believe that
the sun has risen: not only because I see it, but
because by it I see everything else."

—C. S. Lewis

I began this book with a story, so I'll end it with one, too.

Many years ago, when I was still in my twenties and only
a fledgling Christian, I got the opportunity to go to Rome
to write an article for a local newspaper about a conference
that was taking place at the Vatican. Even though it was
only a three-day trip, I jumped at the chance. After all, it
was Rome.

But from the moment I left New York, I felt like I was
on the proverbial trip from hell. I was in the very last row

of seats on the plane, squeezed in between two very large individuals, one of whom spent the entire eight-hour flight snoring so loudly I thought the vibrations might make the engine fall off the wing. I didn't get so much as a minute's sleep, and by the time we landed in Rome I felt like a zombie.

I pretty much stayed that way the next three days, never fully recuperating from the jet lag. It didn't matter much anyway, because the conference was on some theological topic I wasn't very interested in, and all the speakers were way above my head. It would have been a struggle to keep my eyes open even if I hadn't been so tired. To make matters worse, I was staying in a tiny, cramped pensione in the Trastevere section of Rome, which would have been very charming if the weather hadn't been so hot and sticky and the room had been equipped with an air conditioner— which it wasn't.

Anyway, after the two-day conference ended, I had one afternoon free. Just one afternoon to spend by myself in the Eternal City. I was determined to make the most of it. But just as I was about to depart my room, the sky turned the deepest charcoal purple I had ever seen and it started to rain.

Only it wasn't just any rain. It was a storm of biblical proportions. There were flashes of lightning, explosions of thunder, and sheets of solid water pouring down. I stood in the open doorway in disbelief. This was supposed to be "sunny Italy." There hadn't been one cloud in the sky the last two days. And now, just as I was about to enjoy a final few hours before the long plane ride back to New York—*this*?

I was depressed, but I made a decision to go anyway. I grabbed an old, beat-up green umbrella that was lying in the hallway and left. I walked over a tiny, ancient bridge from Trastevere into the historic section of Rome, with the rain coming down in torrents on the Tiber River behind me. I headed north toward the Colosseum, but the gloomy, low-hanging clouds made even that imposing structure too obscure to see. I hadn't brought any casual clothes with me because I knew the conference would take up so much of my time, so I still had on my suit and tie. By now they were soaked clear through to my skin and my leather shoes were ruined. They were so full of water they made a squeaking sound every time they hit the wet, black cobblestone streets.

I have to admit, I was in a wretched mood. The streets were packed with horn-blowing taxis and a few times I even felt like I was back in Manhattan. Finally I turned left and headed up the Via della Pilotta, past cafés and *gelateria*s and ancient churches and palaces, and ducked into a little side street to escape the wind that was blowing in my face. I got lost in the maze of narrow streets and was about to just give up and go back to the pensione to pack when I came out, quite unexpectedly, on the Piazza di Trevi. There, looming high and huge in front of me, was the magnificent Trevi Fountain.

I was tired from all the walking I had done, so I sat down in front of the fountain on one of the low iron railings that surround it. I looked at the Baroque columns and the fearsome figure of Neptune rising from the sea on his chariot of horses. It was still raining so hard that it was difficult to distinguish between the water that was cascading from the fountain and the rain that was pouring down from the sky onto the stone façade. It all seemed to be one colossal font of streaming water. Then it suddenly struck me. I was all alone there. Not a single soul was in the piazza—not one tourist, not one shopkeeper.

Now, anyone who has ever visited Rome knows what an absolute impossibility that is. There are always hundreds of people in front of the Trevi Fountain. *Always*. It doesn't matter what time of day or night it is, or how bad the weather. It's always teeming with people.

But somehow, some way, this wild summer storm had driven everyone out. I looked around me, astonished. It was surreal to be there alone. I felt I was in some kind of Fellini movie and realized that, for just a few moments in time, I actually had this incredible place—this wonder of the world—all to myself.

Surprisingly, the rain didn't bother me anymore. In fact, I knew instinctively that the experience was somehow *better* because of it. The gray-white stone of the statues in the fountain gleamed like armor. And while the clouds had darkened the piazza itself, the rain had caused everything around me to glisten and sparkle. As Chesterton once said, the beauty of rainy weather is that, while the amount of direct light is lessened, the number of things that reflect light is increased. So while there may not be as much sunshine, there are far more lustrous, shiny things.

Sitting there, looking at all the different shapes, shadows, and images, I noticed the reflection of the statues in the pool of the fountain. They seemed to be suspended there, hanging upside down, almost as if they were part of some mysterious dual universe I was looking down into. As I listened to the rain hit the water, my imagination took hold of me, and for one brief instant, it really did seem as if all of history were passing in front of me; it really did seem as if ancient Rome, and the Middle Ages, and the Renaissance, and Christianity were all contained in that one reflecting pool.

And then I had an insight; you might even say I had a vision. I had read Thomas Aquinas and some other theologians, and had accepted Christianity as the most plausible explanation for the questions I had about life. But now, sitting alone in the rain, the water pouring down on my head, I saw something more deeply than ever before. I saw that there really are two worlds—one visible, and one invisible;

one material, and one spiritual. I saw the awesome grandeur of God, who has given us both; I saw the utter absurdity of the atheist position—that all this beauty and wisdom and history that surrounded me had just fallen out of the sky like random drops of rain. I saw why so many people are confused, and I felt sorry for them. Because it really can be confusing to look at all the images reflected by the light of the world, some of them so dazzling they can even make you forget to look up and appreciate the magnificent reality of the light itself.

And I thought about Rome as well, and my disappointing three-day trip. Sitting there among the ancient ruins, I realized that the whole experience was a metaphor for something much bigger. For Rome really was spectacular and beautiful—but it really was in ruins, too. Its greatness, like the greatness of our own human nature and the world itself, was fallen, and in need of redemption and restoration.

That was the key to everything, I thought. I had only just recently become reacquainted with my faith, and I had no idea what joys and sufferings lay ahead. But it didn't matter. I saw now that all of life was an adventure, because all of life was about facing storms and overcoming obstacles and helping repair a fallen, broken world, as we make our way back home—to heaven. And all of life was a romance, because all of life was about falling in love with God.

That was the insight I had sitting there in front of the Trevi Fountain so long ago. It would have been nice if the rain had stopped miraculously and the sun shone through the clouds to confirm it—but it didn't. It just kept pouring down. After a while, I got up and walked back to my hotel in the rain.

But I was no longer depressed. I was joyful.

Acknowledgments

I would like to express my gratitude to all the folks at the Hachette Book Group for the help they've given me—especially Rolf Zettersten, senior vice president of Center Street and FaithWords; Harry Helm, vice president of marketing; and most important, Kate Hartson, my wonderful and brilliant editor. Thank you!

Reading Group Guide

A Travel Guide to Life

1. What two world views does the author point out—one espoused by atheists, and the other by those who believe in God?
2. Why does the author claim that most people are "asleep"?
3. What are some of the things people can do to "wake up" in life?
4. Why do people need to stop complaining?
5. What is the message God gave to St. Paul when he started to complain about his afflictions, and does that message still apply to us today and the problems that we face?
6. What are some of the problems you need to stop complaining about?
7. Why do people need to be honest about themselves and their shortcomings?
8. What three "selves" does the author describe? If you had to list the characteristics of your own three "selves," what would they be?

9. According to the author, what are the four basic foundational pillars on which a consistently happy life can be built?

10. Human beings are a combination of what three things?

11. What function does *the will* play in how the human person is integrated, and why is it impossible for people to compartmentalize their behavior for very long?

12. In general, is what you're doing today moving you closer to where you want to be tomorrow?

13. What are the areas in your life where you need to do an "about face"?

14. What is the principle of inertia, and how does it apply to life in general? In what ways does it apply to *your* life?

15. Why is momentum so important? How might you harness the power of momentum in the different areas of your life that need improvement?

16. What does the author claim is the biggest flaw of the personal development industry, and why?

17. What is the simple answer to the following three questions: Where did we come from? Where are we going? What is life about?

18. What are four simple actions people can take to regain control of their lives when they're feeling overwhelmed by problems?

19. What is the first thing you should do in the morning when you wake up?

20. What is the last thing you should do at night before going to bed?

21. What are some ways you might put God first in your life?

22. Why is physical movement so important?

23. Where in your weekly schedule can you find three thirty-minute blocks of time that you can devote to easy aerobic exercise? How can you make this period less boring and more enjoyable?

24. Why does the author claim that "God is a God of Order"?

25. Explain why sin always causes disorder in our lives.

26. List all the disorderly areas in your life that you are going to clean up, one mess at a time.

27. What is the great "shortcut" to solving the personal problems that St. James spoke about in his epistle?

28. Why is the tongue like the rudder of a ship?

29. Explain what the two following Latin expressions mean, and how they might help you keep your life in perspective:

    • *Memento Mori*
    • *Quid Hoc Ad Aeternitatem*

30. List the different kinds of speech you need to work on cleaning up.

31. Why is faith a decision and not just a feeling?

32. Why is it necessary—not optional—to make a decision about having faith in God?

33. What is comparison morality? Have you ever used it in your own life?

34. How does sinning divide us on three levels?

35. How is forgiveness different from healing?

36. Why does the author compare true faith in God to a bird?

37. What does forgiving people entail—and what doesn't it entail?

38. Make a list of all the people who have wronged you in the past and make a decision to forgive them *now*.

39. Why do you think Cicero called gratitude the "parent" of all virtues?

40. Make a list of all the things in life you are grateful for.

41. What are the things you are *most* grateful for and will commit to thanking God for every day?

42. What is spiritual gravity, or concupiscence, and how does it tie in to the story of the Fall of Adam and Eve?

43. Why is it so important to "stomp on" the sinful temptations you experience when they are still small?

44. What is the D and D system of dealing with moral failures?

45. What does the acronym H.A.L.T. stand for and how does it apply to addictive behavior?

46. When it comes to health matters, what two extremes should be avoided?

47. What are the four main factors that affect a person's health and longevity, and what steps can you take in each area to improve your life?

48. When it comes to money matters, what two extremes should be avoided?

49. According to the author, what are five common-sense steps you can take to begin eliminating financial stress from your life?

50. How should a person go about setting goals in a way that is both humanly effective and spiritually intelligent?

51. In each area of your life—family/relationships, career/vocation, possessions/travels, skills/hobbies, etc.—make a list of what you really want, and *why* you want it.

52. Under each of the goals you listed in your answer to the previous question, make a list of action items you might take towards achieving it.

53. What are the "powers and principalities" that St. Paul spoke about, and what is the evidence that they exist in the world?

54. Why do personal development and self-help techniques often fail us when we are forced to confront evil?

55. What are some of the spiritual weapons we can use to fight against evil?

56. According to the author, when a person experiences intense suffering, what is the only way of dealing with it that really works? Do you agree?

57. What does Christianity say Heaven will be like? Meditate on this for five minutes a day, for the remainder of time you are reading and studying this book.

58. If "love" is really all you need to be happy, why does the author say so many people in the world are unhappy?

59. What is the true definition of love, and what is the greatest symbol for it?

60. What are some of the specific ways you can practice true love in your life?

61. Does the author think that perfect happiness is something that can be achieved in this life? Why or why not?

62. What is the only definitive failure in life?

63. What verse from Psalm 127 sums up this entire book, and why?

64. Why does the author think that all of life is an adventure—and also a romance?

65. Now that you've finished reading this book, what concrete steps can you take to make sure you will begin implementing the most important things you've learned?